Political Leadership in India

**McGill Studies in Development
A Series of the Centre for
Developing-Area Studies,
McGill University**

The Centre for Developing-Area Studies was established at McGill University in the fall of 1963. It fosters interdisciplinary research on problems of economic, social, and political change in the developing countries. Fellowships are awarded annually to graduate students seeking advanced degrees in this field. The Centre offers a program of seminars in development and maintains a specialized library of relevant materials in the social sciences. In addition, the Centre participates in programs of technical cooperation with universities, governments, and other institutions in the developing world.

Previously published in this series:

NATIONALISM AND ECONOMIC DEVELOPMENT IN GHANA
by Roger Genoud

PRAEGER SPECIAL STUDIES IN
INTERNATIONAL POLITICS AND PUBLIC AFFAIRS

Political Leadership in India

AN ANALYSIS OF ELITE ATTITUDES

Michael Brecher

Published in cooperation with the
Centre for Developing-Area Studies,
McGill University

FREDERICK A. PRAEGER, Publishers
New York · Washington · London

The purpose of the Praeger Special Studies is to make specialized research monographs in U.S. and international economics and politics
available to the academic, business, and government communities. For
further information, write to the Special Projects Division, Frederick
A. Praeger, Publishers, 111 Fourth Avenue, New York, N.Y. 10003.

This book is Volume 2 in the series *McGill Studies in Development*.

FREDERICK A. PRAEGER, PUBLISHERS
111 Fourth Avenue, New York, N.Y. 10003, U.S.A.
5, Cromwell Place, London S.W.7, England

Published in the United States of America in 1969
by Frederick A. Praeger, Inc., Publishers

Library of Congress Catalog Card Number: 69-19322

Printed in the United States of America

ACKNOWLEDGMENTS

Two persons contributed much to this project. Dr. John Kurien, an economics colleague at McGill University, drafted the Questionnaire with skill (see Appendix A), after a few intensive discussions with the author had clarified the main topics to be explored. He also read the analysis with care and made valuable comments. Janice Gross Stein, a political science colleague, provided valuable assistance in the task of drawing together the major analytic themes from the welter of data, both within each section and in the over-all conclusions. The coding and computation of the raw data were competently carried out by Koichi Kubota, a Ph.D. candidate in economics at McGill University.

Finally, I am indebted to the Centre for Developing-Area Studies at McGill. It made this study possible by a grant for travel and research. The manuscript was carefully edited, with much benefit to the final product, by Miss Rosalind Boyd, the Centre's editor. And during its brief existence, this Centre has fostered an atmosphere conducive to on-going social science research on developing societies.

McGill University   February, 1968
Montreal

v

CONTENTS

LIST OF TABLES

Table

Chapter 5

CHAPTER **1**

INTRODUCTION

The Fourth General Election constitutes a watershed in the politics of independent India. From 1947 to 1967, the Congress exercised a monopoly of political authority at the center and in all the states, except in Kerala for a few years. India's was truly a one-plus party system, comprising a massive majority party and a number of small opposition groups in the wilderness, that is, groups that could not reasonably expect to assume authority in the foreseeable future. All this changed with the elections of 1967 — from a rather static distribution of political power at the state and all-India levels to a new dynamic equilibrium; from a hegemonial Congress position in Parliament to that of a bare majority; from a near-monopoly of Congress authority in the states to a fragmentation of control, dispersed among eight non-Congress governments. In short, India moved from a one-plus party system to an embryonic multiparty system. Moreover, the first "natural" succession contest occurred in the aftermath of the 1967 elections, as the incumbent Head of Government competed with an older and more senior Congress leader for the post of Prime Minister. The two preceding succession contests (1964, 1966) had been created by the death of the national leader and had been profoundly influenced by that setting. Thus the 1967 contest also marks a divide in India's political development, a challenge to stability during a period of dramatic change in the system.

The Fourth General Election provided a valuable laboratory for behavioral research. Many aspects are being explored by political scientists, Indian and Western. There is great emphasis on electoral attitudes, opinions, and choices, particularly at the constituency level, but at state and all-India levels as well.[1] Other studies concern the selection process for Congress candidates in parliamentary and Assembly seats,[2] and the consequences of the election results for India's political system.[3] An analysis of the 1967 succession contest,

[1] The most comprehensive project of this type was carried out in Kerala — before and after the elections — by the Centre for the Study of Developing Societies in New Delhi.

[2] By Professor W.H. Morris-Jones, Director of the Institute of Commonwealth Studies, University of London.

[3] By various American and Indian scholars.

along with a comparison of the three succession struggles for the Prime Ministership, was undertaken by this writer.[4] In the plethora of research projects, however, there are no inquiries into perceptions and attitudes of members of India's élite groups during this critical transition phase. The study which follows was designed in part to fill this gap; it was also directed at the gathering of data about decision-making in the succession contest of 1967.

The focus of attention throughout this study is *élite images and opinions* about various facets of India's political system. There are three main areas of investigation, through the technique of a structured questionnaire.

Causes and Results of the Congress Setback in the Fourth General Election

This includes élite perceptions of the general and specific causes of Congress reverses at the polls, at the center and in the states; of the continuity of any charismatic role in voter behavior; of Mrs. Indira Gandhi's electoral appeal; of probable results; and of the consequences of the election outcome on the balance of influence within the Congress — between the party hierarchy and parliamentary wing, among geographic groups in the Party, between the Working Committee and Chief Ministers, between the Congress President and other loci of power, personal and institutional. This section also examines élite images of the impact of the election results on the candidates for Prime Minister.

Qualities of Leadership and the Ranking of Congress Leaders

This explores opinions of the élite respondents about the requisite qualities for a good Prime Minister of India in the circumstances of 1967 and of ranking, along a scale of 1 to 4, of the four best-known Congress leaders — Mrs. Gandhi, Morarji Desai, Y.B. Chavan, and K. Kamaraj; fifteen criteria or qualities of leadership were used to secure the assessment of strengths and

---

4 See "Succession in India 1967: The Routinization of Political Change," *Asian Survey*, Vol. VII, No. 7 (July, 1967), pp. 423-43.

weaknesses of the Congress leaders — national image, international image, holding Congress together, maintaining North-South unity, acceptance by the minorities, effective leadership, strong leadership, flexible leadership, ability to deal with the Opposition in Parliament, ability to deal with the states, maintaining harmony with Congress leaders, the likely implementation of a socialist program, providing a better climate for business, the ability to solve economic problems, and the pursuit of a successful foreign policy.

The Succession Contest of 1967

This includes views of the altered date of election of the Congress Parliamentary Party (CPP) Leader — causes of the change, decision-makers of the change, effects on candidates' prospects, and the effect on group influence within the Congress. It also examines opinions on Mrs. Gandhi's selection as Prime Minister in 1966; on the appropriate method of selecting a Prime Minister; on the actual method employed in 1964, 1966, and 1967; on the consistency of choice; on the expectations of the outcome if there had been a secret ballot; on the extent and character of communication and consultation by participants in the 1967 process; and on the initiative taken by participants. Finally, this section probes opinions on the new Cabinet and the prospect for a full term in office and for center-state relations.

There are various intellectually valid conceptions of *élite*. In this study the designation, "formal and informal decision-makers," is the common and basic criterion; but not all groups within that designation are included in the sample. Only three specialized élites are represented — political, academic, and journalist (or opinion leaders). The political group is stressed because of the explicit foci of inquiry in this study — the Fourth General Election and the political process of selection of India's Prime Minister. The inclusion of other élite groups — military, civil service, and business — would be desirable but is of lesser importance. A more basic reason for their exclusion was the severe limitation on time and resources available for field work on this project — less than one month and one interviewer, the writer himself.

The research value of élite interviews is substantial, especially in exploring an élite-dominated political process, such as the selection of a party leader and Head of Government. For one thing, they provide insight into the conscious behavior of those who make decisions, and in this instance the choice of CPP Leader rested with Congress members of Parliament (MPs) and with those who could exert influence on the parliamentarians, notably the organizational leaders of the Congress Working Committee and state chief ministers. Secondly, élite interviews illuminate images and attitudes that enter into élite decisions, and in 1967, the respondents' perception of the causes of the Congress setback at the polls sheds light on the acts (of omission and commission) by Congress leaders which contributed to the debacle. Thirdly, the candid ranking of Congress leaders by élite respondents offers the most accurate prediction of *probable outcome* had there been a secret ballot in the choice of CPP Leader. And in the elaborative comments, freely offered, the interviewees furnished guides to rooted convictions and preferences about many features of the political system. The value of such interviews is greatly enhanced by their paucity, indeed their virtual nonexistence in research studies of Indian politics. Preoccupation with mass electoral behavior, undoubtedly of great value, has led to indifference to élite behavior and the associated images and attitudes that give rise to such behavior. Yet there are certain processes and decisions in Indian politics, as in all politics, which are totally or overwhelmingly dependent on perceptions and choices of small numbers of persons within the system.

One cannot be certain about the truthfulness of articulated images and attitudes. Yet the interviews which form the basis of this study seem to be of a high order of honesty. This judgment is based partly on fifteen years of direct interviewing contact with members of diverse Indian élite groups and the attentive public. It is also based upon the mannerisms of the respondents, the ample character of replies among those who did reply, the candor of many comments, the ease with which some declared that they would answer some questions but not others, the apparent trust in the interviewer's assurance that their names would not be divulged and, most of all, the immediate and cooperative reply to the request for interviews.

None was arranged in advance, for the decision to undertake this project was made only a few days before departure, just after the results of the Fourth General Election were announced. There was no time to secure interviews by mail; nor is that the Indian way. The technique employed was a telephone inquiry, at the end of each day in New Delhi, from March 11 to 28, 1967. For each succeeding day an average of five appointments were made. The interviews were held either in the Central Hall or elsewhere in Parliament, or at the residence of the respondent. Only 2 persons with whom an interview was sought declined — because of lack of time; both were cabinet ministers. Only one, a Congress MP, refused to answer most questions and showed extreme nervousness throughout the interview; he had been appointed a deputy minister between the time he consented to an interview and the time we met. One person expressed an unwillingness to answer "personal" questions but replied to all others. Some respondents declined to answer certain questions; for example, 9 out of the 80 did not engage in the ranking of the Congress leaders' qualities of leadership — but 71 did so. In short, of 82 interviews sought, 80 were actually held; and these persons answered the overwhelming majority of questions. There was also an unsuccessful attempt to see a few more chief ministers, but time did not permit travel outside Delhi.

All but one of the 80 interviews were conducted by the writer, between March 12 and 29, 1967; the other was done by a Canadian graduate student in Delhi, Herbert Fraser. Each interview averaged slightly more than 1 hour; many lasted 1-1/2 hours; none was less than 40 minutes. The candor was gratifying and somewhat unexpected, for the interviews took place during a period of great outcry at the United States' intrusion into Indian affairs, resulting from the disclosures of CIA financial aid to various Indian institutions. One can only surmise that the writer's Canadian identity facilitated cooperation. On the whole, the respondents were very knowledgeable and articulate, though there were exceptions. All spoke English, the language in which the interviews were conducted. Some were surprised by the directness of the questions but most persons adjusted quickly. Many offered lengthy and informative elaborative comments. The pervasive tone was a willingness — in some cases, an undisguised desire — to share attitudes and knowledge about the General Election and the third succession contest. To all who readily consented to an interview and who gave freely of their time and insight, the author is profoundly grateful; without their cooperation, this study would not have been possible.

The sample is not of the random type. It grew out of the initial research focus on the contest for the Prime Ministership in the spring of 1967. Thus it was decided to include both governmental and organizational leaders of the Congress, i.e., cabinet ministers and members of the Working Committee. Because of their role as electors of the CPP Leader, Congress MPs were also included, and because of their influence, state chief ministers. It was also considered appropriate to include a few defeated and ex-Congress leaders or MPs because of the widespread schisms that occurred just before the General Election. To round off political élite representation, one leader from each of the seven Opposition parties in the Lok Sabha was included. Among the opinion leaders, nine prominent commentators and journalists in Delhi were selected, and with them, two foreign correspondents with long residence in India. Finally, six professors at Delhi University and the Indian School of International Studies were added. The distribution by group will be found in Table 1.

TABLE 1

CLASSIFICATION OF RESPONDENTS

Politicians		63
Congress MPs	36	
Congress Cabinet Ministers	6	
Congress Working Committee	8	
Congress State Chief Ministers	2	
Defeated, Denied or ex-Congress MPs	4	
Opposition Party Leaders	7	
Academics		6
Opinion Leaders		11
Indian Journalists	9	
Foreign Journalists	2	
TOTAL		80

The choice of interviewees was made partly in terms of availability and partly in terms of the writer's knowledge of their representative character, based upon many years of field research in India. Thus, the 36 Congress *MPs* constituted one eighth of the total number of Congress parliamentarians in March, 1967; they include 2 from every state of the union, except Kerala and Madras (1 each, because of their decimated contingent in Parliament) and Uttar Pradesh, i.e, UP (4), and Madhya Pradesh, Maharashtra, Bihar, and Jammu and Kashmir (3 each, all but the last because of their size). They are not a random sample but they include all geographic groups; moreover, 11 of the 36 sit in the *Rajya Sabha* (Council of States), the Upper House of Parliament. As for the Congress leaders, the combined number of *Cabinet Ministers and Working Committee members* (14) constitute almost 40 per cent of those two bodies. The state leaders are, however, grossly underrepresented. So too are the *Academics;* and no attempt is made to regard the attitudes of these two latter groups as representative. The Indian *Journalists,* by contrast, include the best-known and the most influential in Delhi. Thus, whatever trends or conclusions are derived from the data do not represent *the élite;* they constitute the attitudes and images of *Indian élite respondents.*

CHAPTER **2**

THE FOURTH GENERAL ELECTION:
CAUSES OF THE CONGRESS SETBACK

TABLE 2 : 1

ELITE ASSESSMENT OF THE CONGRESS SETBACK
IN THE 1967 GENERAL ELECTION

RESPONDENT INITIATED FACTORS

Question: *What do you think are the major factors that account for the failure of the Congress to do as well in this election as in the previous one?*

	Congress MPs	Others	Total	Percentage of Total
Economic Problems	14	16	30	38.
Desire For Change	6	9	15	19.
United Opposition	1	5	6	7.5
Internal Quarrels	1	1	2	2.5
Corruption	1	0	1	1.25
Lack of Effective Leadership	1	0	1	1.25
Other	12	12	24	30.
TOTAL	36	43[a]	79	100.

[a]One Indian Journalist explicitly refused to cite *any* factors in all-India terms; thus a total of 43 instead of 44 non-Congress MP respondents.

Two factors stand out in the response to this initial question about the election results: Thirty-eight per cent of the persons interviewed cited *Economic Problems* as the principal cause of Congress losses at the polls; half as many perceived an intangible *Desire for Change* as the most important reason for the setback. Four other specified causes — *United Opposition, Internal Quarrels, Corruption, and Lack of Effective Leadership* — accounted for an additional 12.5 per cent. Measured in ratio terms, the over-all Rank 1 frequency of Economic Problems relative to Desire for Change relative to the four lesser factors combined is 3 to 1.5 to 1.

The weight of Congress MPs and Others in the over-all Rank 1 frequency of Economic Problems is almost equal; in the Desire for Change, the weight of Others is slightly greater (21 per cent of all Others and 16.6 per cent of all MPs). *The breakdown by groups reveals the greatest contrast to be between political and nonpolitical respondents – in both of the major factors.* Congress rank-and-file MPs and Congress leaders displayed a virtually equal stress on Economic Problems – 38 and 36 per cent respectively. Opposition leaders and Defeated, Disillusioned, and Ex-(DDE) Congressmen showed the same degree of emphasis, 36 per cent. Yet, not a single Academic regarded economic discontent as the key factor. The balance is corrected somewhat by the Journalists: Five of the 9 cited Economic Problems as the crucial cause of Congress electoral reverses. In the case of Desire for Change, the balance of emphasis between political and nonpolitical respondents is reversed: Only 6 of the 36 MPs and 2 of the 14 Congress leaders, along with 1 of the 11 among the Opposition and DDE groups, ranked this first, i.e., 9 of the 61; but 4 of the 6 Academics and 3 of the 9 Journalists did so, a comparison of 15 per cent (political respondents) and 47 per cent (nonpolitical).

Among Congress MPs, the pre-eminence of these two factors is clear: No other cause of election reverses received Rank 1 from more than one respondent. Among the Cabinet Ministers, first in importance was attributed to four factors – Economic Problems and United Opposition, 2 each, and Internal Quarrels and Desire for Change, 1 each. Working Committee respondents cited three factors as most important – Economic Problems (3), United Opposition (2), and Desire for Change (1). The only other factor to be given primacy by more than 2 respondents was United Opposition, with 6, i.e., 4 Congress leaders, 1 MP and 1 Academic. In short, *a substantial plurality perceived economic discontent as the prime explanation of the election outcome; and two thirds of the élite sample cited three factors – Economic Problems, Desire for Change, and United Opposition.*

TABLE 2 : 2

ELITE ASSESSMENT OF THE CONGRESS SETBACK
IN THE 1967 GENERAL ELECTION

RESPONDENT INITIATED FACTORS

RANKED IN ORDER OF IMPORTANCE

	Congress MPs	Others	Total
Economic Problems			
First factor	14	16	30
Second factor	11	14	25
Third factor	2	6	8
Fourth factor	2	1	3
Desire for Change			
First factor	6	9	15
Second factor	3	1	4
Third factor	2	0	2
Fourth factor	1	1	2
United Opposition			
First factor	1	5	6
Second factor	2	3	5
Third factor	1	4	5
Fourth factor	0	6	6
Internal Quarrels			
First factor	1	1	2
Second factor	2	6	8
Third factor	7	4	11
Fourth factor	3	1	4
Corruption			
First factor	1	0	1
Second factor	1	6	7
Third factor	1	1	2
Fourth factor	3	2	5
Lack of Effective Leadership, Absence of Charismatic Leader			
First factor	1	0	1
Second factor	1	0	1
Third factor	0	7	7
Fourth factor	0	2	2

(continued)

15

TABLE 2 : 2 — *Continued*

	Congress MPs	Others	Total
Issues Like Cow Slaughter, Language			
First factor	0	0	0
Second factor	1	2	3
Third factor	3	1	4
Fourth factor	0	2	2

A notable feature of the data in Table 2 : 2 is the *variety and multiplicity of factors initiated* by the élite respondents: Ten distinct causes of Congress election losses were cited; these ranged from tangible economic issues, through political traits concerning party unity and leadership, to the intangible Desire for Change; no less than 76 persons mentioned at least 2 factors, 56 initiated 3, and as many as 30 respondents noted 4 factors. *All this indicates sophistication and a mature, pluralist perception among the élite members interviewed.*

The preponderance of Economic Problems, noted earlier, continued along a scale of 4 important factors: It was mentioned by 66 of the 80 respondents, i.e., 82.5 per cent. In aggregate terms, there is a slightly heavier weight of Others in the over-all frequency for this factor (84 per cent of all Others and 80 per cent of Congress MPs). More specifically, all 7 Opposition leaders ranked Economic Problems first or second, while only 25 of the 36 Congress MPs did so — and 7 of them did not even mention it as a cause of the setback. Congress leaders fall in between with respect to high ranking for economic matters — 4 of the 6 Cabinet Ministers and 5 of the 8 members of the Working Committee giving this factor first or second order of importance in the election results. In short, *the Opposition image placed greater emphasis on economic discontent than did the party in power, and Congress leaders were more aware of the role of Economic Problems than the rank-and-file.*

The Desire for Change yields second place in over-all frequency (23) to Internal Quarrels (25), but it must be regarded as second in the general order of importance because of its high Rank 1 occurrence — half of that in Economic Problems and more than double its nearest rival, United Opposition. The weight of Congress MPs is higher than Others in this factor — one third of all MPs mentioned Desire for Change, while only one fourth of all Others did so. More significantly, only 2 of 14 Congress leaders cited this. Thus the ratio of MPs to party leaders who perceived that the country wanted a change was 2.4 to 1. Surprisingly, only 1 of 7 Opposition leaders mentioned this factor. Noteworthy too is the heavy concentration of nonpolitical respondents on this cause: Four of the 6 Academics and 4 of the 9 Journalists mentioned it; 7 of those 8 gave it the highest order of importance. More generally, only 24 per cent of the political respondents mentioned Desire for Change, while 53 per cent of the nonpolitical respondents did so. Thus, *the academic and communications interviewees displayed acute perception of this intangible cause of electoral behavior in India's Fourth General Election; the Congress MPs showed considerable awareness; and the political leaders of all persuasions were hardly conscious that this mood operated in the minds of the Indian electorate.*

Measured by unweighted frequency of occurrence, the other initiated causes of Congress reverses were: Internal Quarrels (25), United Opposition (22), Corruption (15), Lack of Leadership (11), and special Issues (9). Very few Congress MPs (only 4) thought the United Opposition a factor worth noting at all; many more among Others, 18, mentioned this cause; indeed, while only 1 MP gave it the highest ranking, 5 Others did so. Viewed in terms of group perception, only the Academics, 4 of the 6, Opposition leaders, 5 of the 7, and the Congress leaders, 6 out of 14, gave it a high over-all ranking. Merely 4 of the 36 Congress MPs and only 1 of the 9 Journalists noted this factor. Yet 5 of the respondents who gave it first rank belonged to the Congress. Thus, *the élite sample as a whole perceived the factor of United Opposition as inconsequential; yet the Opposition leaders stressed their own influence — as did the Congress leaders to a lesser extent, and the Academics. Further, the image of the governing party's respondents was split between leaders and rank-and-file MPs; so too were the academic and communications interviewees.*

To the inversely related factor of Internal Quarrels, equal attention was given by Congress MPs and Others, though more of the former gave it Rank 3, and more of the latter, Rank 2. Within the Congress there was a marked difference in image: Only slightly more than one third of the MPs mentioned this as a cause, while half of the party leaders did so. The Opposition leaders disregarded it totally. And both the Academics and Journalists perceived it as of little importance. Thus, *only Congress respondents were conscious of the impact of their party's schisms on electoral behavior.*

Corruption has long been an issue of controversy in public discussion within India. To some, it has been an unmitigated evil cutting at the roots of social and political morality. Others regard it as highly exaggerated and no more serious than in the political systems of other democratic states. Still others consider corruption a necessary (and even welcome) lubricant to the decision process in the government of a developing economy. Charges of Congress corruption raged for some years before the 1967 General Election. Not surprisingly, *it was in the minds of élite respondents – and yet with less weight than might have been expected.* Only 1 person, an MP, gave it the highest importance as the cause of Congress setbacks. Only 6 out of 36 MPs mentioned it at all, along with 9 others, altogether less than 20 per cent of the total number of respondents. The distribution was relatively equal among various groups – 1 out of every 6 Congress MPs, 2 of the 14 Congress leaders, 1 of the 7 Opposition leaders. *Only the nonpolitical respondents revealed a deeper imprint of years of allegation and malpractice on élite perception –* 5 of 15, or one third, mentioned corruption as a cause of Congress defeat.

Few of the interviewees considered special Issues like Cow Slaughter or Language of sufficient importance to initiate them as major causes of the election outcome: Only 4 Congress MPs and 5 Others mentioned them along the four-fold scale, none in the first rank. However, a large number acknowledged them as contributory factors in certain states: Cow Slaughter in select northern states, like Harayana, Delhi, UP, and Bihar, and Language in Madras. Slightly greater weight was given to the Lack of Effective (or Charismatic) Leadership: Nine of the 11 references fell in the third or fourth order of importance; 1 Congress MP cited this as the most important factor. On the whole, *Congress MPs were less aware than Others of*

the link between quality of leadership and electoral choice; and all
segments of the élite perceived this factor as marginal.

As noted in Tables 2: 1 and 2: 2, many other factors were cited
as the most important cause (and contributory causes) of the
Congress reverses at the polls. Indeed, the theme of variety and
multiplicity — the pluralist perception of the élite respondents — is
best revealed by a selection from their replies to this introductory
question.

MPs

The twelve "Other" most important factors may be noted first:
"Having come to power, Congress never thought of going to the
masses" *or* its variation,
"We have lost contact with the masses, especially the poor
villagers" (4 occurrences).
"Proper implementation of the Congress program was lacking in
most areas" or a similar phrasing (3 occurrences, along with 1 in
Rank 2, 2 in Rank 3, and 1 in Rank 4).
"Maladministration" (2 occurrences, along with 1 in Rank 3).
"False propaganda of the Opposition parties" (1 occurrence,
along with a variation in Rank 2 — "People are gullible and accepted
Opposition arguments").
"Decline in character and integrity, in conviction and confi-
dence" (1 occurrence); and
"Nature — bad weather" (1 occurrence). "This conspired with
Internal Quarrels to bring about the virtual downfall of Congress."

In addition, there were factors cited in Ranks 2, 3, 4, or more,
some of them cited by a number of respondents:
"Youth was not attracted to Congress — and many new voters
were added since 1962."
"Government was yielding to pressure tactics."
"Complacency in certain states."
"Lack of organizational effort, lack of cohesion, and lack of
purposeful direction."

"Caste and other factors of choosing candidates."

"Newer people came into Congress and were more interested in 'the loaves and fishes of office'."

"People feel planning has not yielded fruit soon enough."

"Business supported the Opposition — Jan Sangh and Swatantra — with a lot of money."

"Many Congress candidates were ignorant or ineffective."

This exercise compels a revision of the analysis of the "most important factor" initiated by Congress MPs. While Economic Problems and Desire for Change retain their position of highest and second highest frequency, three other factors have multiple Rank 1 occurrence — Lack of Contact with the Masses, Improper Implementation, and Maladministration. And if one adds the three "Other" factors with Rank 1 frequency, noted above, there were no less than a dozen distinct factors cited by 36 MP respondents as the most important cause of Congress electoral reverses.

A few other random comments by MPs are worth noting. One declared, "It is not a setback; it shows how democracy in India is working." Another observed, "This time people voted for personalities, not for Congress; after the next General Election, Congress may sit on the Opposition benches." A third saw it in another light: "The electorate exercised a negative vote — against the Congress." And a fourth claimed, "The absence of (Jawaharlal) Nehru meant a loss of an additional 25 to 30 seats in Parliament." No other respondent concurred.

Others

Among the 44 non-Congress MP respondents, more than a third made some elaborative comments of substance, in reply to this initial question about the Fourth General Election.

Cabinet Ministers

One senior minister summed up the election results as "a sort of protest vote arising out of economic troubles in the past two years."

He added, after a brief pause: "We are too near the events and must explore the process; but tentative impressions are possible." Two other members of the cabinet took the position that it is "very difficult" or "impossible" to generalize for India as a whole. Hence, they offered a state-by-state analysis — within an all-India perspective. A summary of each follows:

A. The Congress has done well in Maharashtra, Madhya Pradesh, Andhra and Mysore; in Madras, the losses were due to language and the rice shortage; in Kerala, it was the food shortage, along with schisms in the Congress and the desire to get rid of President's Rule; in Rajasthan, it was the role of the feudal order; in Punjab, the *Akali* factor was responsible; in the UP, it was a combination of weak leadership and the lack of Muslim support, the latter due to the Urdu question and the agitation over Aligarh University. ("Lack of faith by the minorities" was cited by this respondent as the third of 4 general causes of the setback at the polls.) And in Bihar, it was weak leadership, along with the food shortage and the police firing in Patna. No other states were mentioned. Yet in general, he added, "The election results in 1967 were not much worse than in 1962."

B. Only a few states were mentioned by this minister; the focus was rather on the key factors. Thus, Internal Quarrels wreaked havoc in the UP and Bihar; the Lack of Effective Leadership in Orissa, where "Government broke down"; the United Opposition and, to a small extent, Language, in Madras; Cow Slaughter in North India, and, for the rest, general causes, notably the Desire for Change and the loss of contact with youth. "Even with Nehru," he added, "the results would have been bad." He warned that the country "will have to go through a period of wildness — but Congress will stage a comeback, if economic conditions improve."

There was only one other person who offered a state-by-state analysis, a prominent Indian Journalist. (Two MPs also said, "different reasons for different states" but they did not elaborate.) In Madras, he stated that Congress is identified with the North — "It was a gesture of assertion against northern domination; Congress will come back or the *Dravida Munnetra Kazhagam* (DMK) will change its character; language was secondary"; in Kerala, Congress "blundered by exploiting communal groups"; in West Bengal, Congress "began to be identified with the monopoly section of big business in Calcutta; the rejection of Congress is a rejection of non-Bengali big money"; in Orissa, the rejection of Congress "was due to the displacement of most experienced Congress politicians like (Bijoyanand) Patnaik"; in Bihar and the UP, "it was completely due to in-fighting — in Bihar, to caste factionalism, and in the UP, to a power struggle"; and in the Punjab and Haryana, Congress lost because of the division of the state. "The results," he concluded, "were not an all-India integrated phenomenon."

Working Committee Members

For one organizational leader, the most important cause of the setback was that "moneyed interests were against Congress because of its socialist platform." Another member of the "High Command" also cited this, but as a contributory factor. He added, "U.S. money was involved"; no one else echoed this theme. Perhaps the most pungent comments of all 80 respondents came from still another member of the Committee regarding

Economic Problems: "People were disgusted by the stupidities — the overstress on ideologies."

Corruption: "Proved corruption in High Places, many Chief Ministers, though not all."

Internal Quarrels: "The formation of the Jana Congress was unnecessary and avoidable."

Cow Slaughter: "Responsible for 10 per cent of Congress losses."

Lack of Leadership: "There has been no leader since Nehru of any quality."

Minorities: "Nearly 80 per cent of the Muslims voted against Congress — on secret instructions from Pakistan."

"The debacle," he concluded, "was due to Government — and, as Prime Minister, Mrs. Gandhi must take her share of the responsibility."

Opposition Leaders

One respondent put it bluntly in citing Economic Problems as the key factor: "Basically people think of their stomach"; and, as for Corruption, "it was literally down to the grass roots, a feeling that everyone has a price." Another person remarked: "The image of Congress in the past twenty years has been badly damaged – to the point of the 'ugly Congressman'; Congress became the symbol of failure in every field of life; there is a feeling of sickness with Congress." A third Opposition leader made a sweeping condemnation of the Congress record: "It did not fulfill the expectations in the minds of the people; Congress has not solved any problem facing the country – food, language, foreign relations; we have been drifting from crisis to crisis."

Academics

Three of the Academics made general observations of interest on the election results. One stressed the widespread discontent: "Generally people were fed up with Congress, particularly at the state level; they were fed up with corruption, jobbery, and nepotism, and there was an impression it was there on a large scale." Another cited as the most important factor, "People were sick of old faces, old bosses, and an aged party." He also paid tribute to the "unconscious grapevine of the electorate" which cut down many Congress bosses in different parts of the country. And he concluded on an optimistic note about the meaning of the Fourth General Election: "The maturity and articulation of the electorate is the greatest hope of the future – the new force. No one can hereafter ignore the electorate." Still another Academic offered a thoughtful general explanation for the setback: "In a country like India, the ruling party is always at a disadvantage – expectations are growing, and the party's shortcomings will always be increasingly apparent; by 1962, only the Goa stunt staved off defeat; by 1967, much had crumbled, the China defeat, etc." And he added a shrewd comment on the impact of the communications network: "If the forecasts of reverses had been known earlier, the Congress organization would have responded." Only half in jest, one Academic stressed the pervasiveness of Internal Quarrels: "Just as every Indian has a caste, every Congressman has a faction."

Journalists

The extensive state-by-state analysis by one Journalist has already been noted. Another introduced a novel factor into the discussion: "The prestige of the Congress declined with the loss of India's international prestige." A third was sceptical about the notion of a United Opposition: "If they had been really united, they would have thrown the Congress out." The same respondent was the only person to cite as a factor, "the element of Hindu revivalism in the country."

In general, the scope of comment and analysis is impressive for a small segment of India's élites, revealing insight of a high order on the whole.

TABLE 2 : 3

ELITE ASSESSMENT OF THE CONGRESS SETBACK
IN THE 1967 GENERAL ELECTION

INTERVIEWER'S SUGGESTED FACTORS

Question: *Are the following factors, not mentioned by you in your initial comments, additional causes of the Congress setback?* (Each factor was mentioned individually to each respondent.)

	Congress MPs	Others	Total
Internal Quarrels	18	21	39
Lack of Effective Leadership	15	18	33
United Opposition	14	12	26
Issues Like Cow Slaughter	19	27	46
Absence of Charismatic Leadership	19	20	39
Economic Problems	7	2	9

If one combines Initiation and Responsiveness for these six factors, on the basis of a simple frequency count, the results are as follows:

TABLE 2 : 4

ELITE ASSESSMENT OF THE CONGRESS SETBACK
IN THE 1967 GENERAL ELECTION

RESPONDENT INITIATED AND ACCEPTED FACTORS

	Initiation	Responsiveness	Total[a]	Not Mentioned	Rank
Internal Quarrels	26[b]	39	65	15	2
Lack of Effective Leadership	7[c]	33	40	40	6
United Opposition	22	26	48	32	4
Issues Like Cow Slaughter	10[b]	46	56	24	3
Absence of Charismatic Leadership	5[c]	39	44	36	5
Economic Problems	67[b]	9	76	4	1

[a] This combined count is designated as the *recognition* scale.
[b] The discrepancy between these figures and the totals expressed in Table 2:2 is due to the fact that one initiating reference to each of these fell beyond the fourth factor in order of importance.
[c] The two leadership factors were derived from a tabulation of the primary data.

Given the high proportion of interviewees who cited Economic Problems in their initial comment, the pre-eminence of this factor in the over-all ranking is not unexpected. *Only 4 of the 80 respondents did not consider food or prices relevant to the election outcome;* this exceptional group consisted of the 2 Chief Ministers, 1 Academic, and 1 Indian Journalist. *The second over-all rank* accorded to *Internal Quarrels* also *corresponds to its prominence in the initiation scale of frequency.* Altogether 80 per cent of the respondents cited or acknowledged its relevance; the 15 persons who did not were representative in the sense that they included all élite categories except the Cabinet. They consisted of 5 Congress MPs, 2 each from the Working Committee, Opposition leaders, and Indian Journalists, and 1 each from the other groups. United Opposition ranks third in the initiation scale but falls to fourth place in the combined count, that is, the *recognition scale.* There is an exchange of rank with special Issues like Cow Slaughter, the latter having a small initiation frequency but very high acknowledgment by the respondents as relevant. With respect to United Opposition, 60 per cent recognized

its relevance; the 40 per cent, who did not, represent all élite groups
except Foreign Journalists.

The breakdown sheds some light on images: Congress MPs
attached the least importance to this factor — 50 per cent did not
mention it; almost half of the interviewed Congress leaders concurred
that it was irrelevant, but a further breakdown reveals dissent among
the Cabinet Ministers — only 1 of the 6 agreed; Indian Journalists,
too, seemed little aware of this factor; but only 1 each among the
Opposition leaders and Academics did not mention it.

In short, *Cabinet Ministers, Opposition leaders, and Academics*
share an image of United Opposition as being highly relevant to the
election results, while Congress MPs, the Working Committee, and
Indian Journalists share an image about half way along the
recognition scale.

The élite perception of the electoral role of special Issues Like
Cow Slaughter and Language is similar to the image of the two
leadership factors. In all three, there is a very wide gap between the
frequency of initiation and of responsiveness — 1 to 4.6 for special
Issues, 1 to 8 for the Absence of Charismatic Leadership, and 1 to
almost 5 for the Lack of Effective Leadership. Measured in terms of
the total number of respondents, the proportion who cited these
factors *before* they were mentioned by the interviewer were,
respectively, 12.5, 9, and 6 per cent, i.e., ranging from small to
marginal. Yet all three were acknowledged to be relevant by many
when the specific focus was injected into the discussion. The
breakdown by group sheds further light. Among four élite groups —
Congress MPs, Working Committee, Opposition leaders, and Foreign
Journalists — approximately half within each responsively acknowledged the relevance of Issues Like Cow Slaughter. The proportion
was much higher for three other groups — Cabinet (5 out of 6),
Academics (5 out of 6), and Indian Journalists (7 out of 9). Yet,
with all that, 30 per cent of the total respondents considered these
issues as irrelevant. And among the persons who acknowledged a
role, almost all agreed that their influence was state-wide — Language
in Madras, and Cow Slaughter in North India, especially in Delhi,
Rajasthan, Harayana, and UP. *Viewed in the aggregate, then, the*
statistical data and the consensus on limited state or régional

influence suggest that the élite as a whole perceived these special Issues as of minor importance in the election outcome. This conclusion is accentuated by the fact that more than 80 per cent of those who did acknowledge their relevance did so responsively; these issues were remote from élite consciousness.

The same basic finding applies to the leadership factors, with even greater emphasis. Almost half of the respondents take no notice of either factor, and of those who do, more than 80 per cent acknowledge their relevance responsively. The proportion is consistently high for all élite groups. Charismatic Leadership was acknowledged by Congress MPs (19 out of 20), Cabinet (3 out of 3), Working Committee (5 out of 6), Opposition leaders (2 out of 3), and Academics and Indian Journalists (3 out of 4). So too with Lack of Effective Leadership: Congress MPs (15 out of 17), Cabinet (2 out of 3), Working Committee (3 out of 4), Academics (3 out of 4), and Indian Journalists (6 out of 6). *Noteworthy among those who denigrated the electoral significance of Charisma were Cabinet Ministers* (3 out of 6 did not mention it), *Opposition leaders* (4 out of 7), and *Indian Journalists* (5 out of 9). As to *Lack of Effective Leadership, Congress leaders* (Cabinet, Working Committee, and Chief Ministers) *and Opposition leaders shared an image that this was of little or no consequence in the election results.*

One final trait may be noted about the initiation and responsiveness (recognition) data. *In two of the six factors, there is a relatively equal frequency of initiation and responsiveness:* Internal Quarrels (26 to 39), and United Opposition (22 to 26). *Among the other four factors, there is a gross imbalance,* heavily in favor of initiation in Economic Problems (67 to 9), and heavily in favor of responsiveness in Issues like Cow Slaughter (10 to 46), Lack of Effective Leadership (7 to 33), and Absence of Charismatic Leadership (5 to 39). Finally, it appears that *the élite as a whole perceived only three factors to be important (among these six) — Economic Problems, Internal Quarrels, and United Opposition. To these may be added the Desire for Change and Corruption.*

Further insight into perceptions held by Congress leaders is provided by the views expressed at the state level soon after the General Election (see Appendix B).

TABLE 3 : 1

SPECIFIC ACTIONS AS CAUSES OF CONGRESS SETBACK
IN THE 1967 GENERAL ELECTION

ACTIONS BY THE GOVERNMENT

Question: *Can you think of any specific action on the part of Government in the past year which has contributed to the decline of the Congress majority in Parliament and the Assemblies?* [a]

	Congress MPs	Others	Total
None	14	13	27
Yes			
Devaluation	19	22	41
Punjab Partition	2	2	4
Cow Riots	3	2	5
Others and DUAC[b]	17	24	41

[a] Multiple answers were permitted.
[b] DUAC includes the answers whose classification is difficult, e.g., do not know, uncertain.

TABLE 3 : 2

SPECIFIC ACTIONS AS CAUSES OF CONGRESS SETBACK
IN THE 1967 GENERAL ELECTION

ACTIONS BY THE CONGRESS PARTY

Question: *Can you think of any specific action on the part of the Congress Party in the past year which has contributed to the decline of the Congress majority in Parliament and the Assemblies?* [a]

	Congress MPs	Others	Total
None	21	21	42
Yes			
Faulty Selection of Candidates	8	9	17
Others and DUAC	8	20	28

[a] Multiple answers were permitted.

It is apparent from the data in Tables 3:1 and 3:2 that *a substantial proportion of élite respondents did not perceive any link between specific acts — of Government or Party — and the election results:* A third expressed this image concerning Government actions, and slightly more than a half regarding Congress actions. In terms of group distribution, the Cabinet and Congress MPs are above average in viewing the irrelevance of Government acts, two thirds and 40 per cent respectively. As for Congress acts, these two groups are joined by Opposition leaders in asserting their electoral irrelevance, with even greater emphasis — 21 of the 36 MPs (i.e., almost 60 per cent), 5 of the 6 Cabinet Ministers, and 6 of the 7 Opposition leaders. In short, *the governing élite* (Cabinet) *emphatically denies electoral significance to any specific acts; the Opposition élite concurs with regard to Party actions, as does the Congress rank-and-file in large measure.* A large majority of those who did not perceive any link remarked that it was the general deterioration in conditions — economic, social, bureaucratic corruption, and other — which caused the electoral protest; so too with the steady decline in the Congress image; specific acts merely accentuated these trends. Not untypical was the remark, "A change in leadership would make no difference; the rot in the Congress had gone too far." One Working Committee member noted: "The High Command did not function during the year — even for the elections; every leader collected his own funds and supported his own candidates."

He added, in words echoing criticism of India's political system from the far Left: "One hundred families control the wealth and newspapers — and were supporting one or another candidate, rather than a party. This is a threat to democracy despite Congress talk of socialism."

Only *one specific act of the Government* was cited by many as a cause of the Congress setback at the polls: Slightly more than half of the respondents mentioned *devaluation* of the rupee in June, 1966. Among the élite groups, Indian Journalists (8 of the 9) and Academics (5 of the 6) were most emphatic on this theme. The Congress rank-and-file and Working Committee leaders stood at the average in tone and frequency of recognition; and at the other extreme were the Opposition leaders (2 of the 7) and the Cabinet (1 of the 6). In short, *the communications élites stressed the impact of devaluation, while the incumbent and competing governing élites denigrated its electoral role.*

One Indian Journalist remarked: "The devaluation decision was right, but without a followthrough it had no benefit." Another observed that it enabled the opposition to stress the lowering of the value of money and the influence of foreign pressure. A third perceived the political effect of devaluation as being confined to "the thinking and business classes in the cities." A fellow commentator, however, claimed wider significance: "It devalued the Congress and the lady herself." The Academics used similar themes: "The way it was handled seriously undermined the image of the Government"; "it caused disunity within the Congress, especially the acrimonious debate within the All-India Congress Committee (AICC)"; and the sweeping remark, "Devaluation and its consequences was the one major disastrous decision taken by Mrs. Gandhi." At the other extreme, three Cabinet Ministers explicitly stated that it had no political consequence. One noted, with greater sophistication, "Specific acts are relevant, but essentially it was the consequence of economic difficulty and the erosion of the will of the government." Most Opposition leaders, as noted, disregarded devaluation. One, however, termed it a "confession of failure by the Congress," and another perceived "the devaluation of values as more important than the devaluation of currency."

The other two specific acts — Punjab Partition and Cow Riots — were mentioned by so few that they may be ignored. Other factors included Cabinet changes, police firing on students, yielding to foreign, notably American, pressure, and the like. To many, however, it was acts of omission that were more significant. One Journalist referred to the "inability to deal with students, *sadhus,* hoarders, or to improve the administration." Another spoke of the paralysis of the government: "There was no government left, only a collection of ministries, and no action on any issue." And a third spoke of "a total misreading of the nature of the period, as one of marking time."

The only *specific Congress act* to warrant attention was the *poor selection of candidates* for the Fourth General Election. As one respondent remarked, "The electorate did what the Congress Central

Election Committee should have done." The Congress rank-and-file and Congress organizational leaders were the most critical groups, but even together they were a distinct minority — 17 out of 80. Most replies fell in the categories of "none" or "don't know"; some reverted to "devaluation" or other acts of government. Indeed, *acts of Government and acts of Party were perceived as synonymous by a majority of the persons interviewed.* This was a "natural" legacy of twenty years of Congress *Raj* but *a disquieting symptom in the élite image — the fusion of two different structures performing different functions in India's political system: The distinction between authoritative rule-making and rule enforcement on the one hand, and interest advocacy and aggregation on the other, was somewhat blurred.*

TABLE 4

ASSESSMENT OF CONTINUITY OF THE CHARISMATIC ROLE
IN VOTER BEHAVIOR

Question: *Do you think Mrs. Gandhi's position as the daugther of Jawaharlal Nehru helped the Congress Party in the Election?*

	Congress MPs	Others	Total	
Yes	18	19	37	
No Further Reply	0	2	2	
Very Much	5	5	10	
Much	2	0	2	
Marginal	11	12	23	
No	17	19	36	
No Further Reply	4	5	9	
Did Hurt	2	0	2	
Did Not Hurt	11	14	25	
DUAC	2	1	3	
No Answer	1	3	4	

Charisma was a conspicuous and influential factor in Indian politics for almost half a century: Gandhi and Nehru displayed it in abundance from 1920 to 1964. The question of its impact on voter behavior in the postcharismatic era is of considerable interest. The data in Table 4 reveal that almost half of the élite respondents (37 out of 80) or, if one excludes the DUAC and "No Answer" groups, slightly more than half perceived that charisma had a positive influence on voters in the 1967 General Election. Only 11 persons said that it did not help the Congress Party—and only 2 considered it a liability. An even sharper focus emerges if one combines the replies, "Yes"—it helped, with "Did not Hurt" and compares this with "Did Hurt": More than 75 per cent of the élite members interviewed saw the charismatic link as an asset or not detrimental; and *the ratio of image of charismatic link as nonliability to liability is 31 to 1.* An alternative ratio may be formulated by combining the replies, "No, No Further Reply," i.e., no—did not help, with "Did not Hurt" and comparing this with "Yes": The results are *relatively equal images of the charismatic link as a neutral influence on voter behavior (34) on the one hand, and as a positive electoral asset (37) on the other.*

Within the "Yes" or asset category, 60 per cent considered this factor of marginal influence, and these respondents, in turn, were equally divided between Congress MPs and Others. Well over half the MPs who viewed the link as helpful with the voters defined it as "Marginal"; other élite groups who stressed the marginal effect were Academics (3 out of 6) and Foreign Journalists (2 out of 2). Only 12 of the 37 perceived it as a substantial asset—"Much" or "Very Much." The 5 Others among them were scattered in Cabinet, Opposition, Academics, and Indian Journalists. The only 2 persons who perceived the link as harmful were Congress MPs. Opposition leaders stood out among the group that declared it did not help (3 of the 9, and 3 of the 7 Opposition leaders interviewed). The other, much larger neutral group—"Did not Hurt"—was widely represented among the élites: There were as many Congress MPs (11) in this category as in the "Marginal" help category, along with Cabinet (2), half the Working Committee group (4), Opposition (3), and Indian Journalists (3). Perhaps *the dominant mood was that Mrs. Gandhi's link with Nehru's charisma was an electoral asset of marginal value; it was certainly not crucial nor the most important factor in voter behavior but it was also not a liability for the Congress in the Fourth Election.*

Few of the Congress MPs elaborated at length upon their basic "Yes" or "No" answer. Only three comments are worth noting. One was an extreme view, completely atypical—"Without Mrs. Gandhi the Congress would have lost the Center." Another was widely shared among the élite respondents — "She drew large crowds, but this did not influence the voting very much." And the third was perceptive about the political relevance of her link with charisma—"of little consequence, but her election as Leader was very much due to this relationship." The Academic respondents were also inarticulate on this point. Among the Congress leaders, members of the Working Committee were more outspoken: Three echoed the theme of "attracting crowds but not votes." One remarked that "the Indian voter is more mature today—he does not vote for a person's position." Another replied, "absolutely none," to the question about help for the party. And one member was less than gallant with the remark, "Not being Nehru's daughter she would have had nothing; she has most of the vices but few of the virtues of her father." Cabinet Ministers were more generous: One stressed that "she is the only national leader who did national campaigning effectively, and she did this in her own right"; and two others remarked that she has greater mass contact than any other Congress leader. *The difference in tone between the two segments of the Congress élite confirms the deep tension between organizational and governmental wings at the all-India level during Mrs. Gandhi's Prime Ministership.*

Among the Opposition leaders only one articulated a view—and this was positive: "A substantial asset, to which she brings certain qualities, modernism, liberalism, and grace." Most pointed were the comments of Indian Journalists. One was complimentary: "She counters the pervasive image of the corrupt, disagreeable Congress politician," but even that did" not necessarily win votes." Another remarked, "Nehru's mantle was partial compensation for her inadequacies as speaker, thinker, and administrator." But the most critical remark of all 80 respondents came from still another Journalist: "If anything, the link had the reverse effect—a serious reflection on the nation that among 500 million people we need a woman to rule, 500 million eunuchs ruled by one woman."

TABLE 5

IMAGE OF ELECTORAL APPEAL OF MRS. GANDHI

Question: *Did you, at any time during the past year (January 1966 to February
1967), think that another Prime Minister would have helped the party
better in the Election ?*
(For those who replied, "yes," the further questions were asked
"when" and "who.")

	Congress MPs	Others	Total
Yes	10	13	23
No	24	26	50
DUAC	1	2	3
No Answer	1	3	4

	Congress MPs	Others	Total
Yes			
At Outset	4	4	8
Devaluation Decision (June, 1966)	0	3	3
Cow Riots (November, 1966)	1	0	1
Others	4	5	9
No Further Reply	1	1	2
Yes			
Morarji Desai	5	7	12
Others, DUAC, No Answer	5	6	11

It is apparent from the data in Table 5 that the composite élite
image of Mrs. Gandhi's electoral appeal remained constant during the
year following her initial selection as Prime Minister. A clear majority
of respondents (50 of the 80) indicated that, throughout the period,
January, 1966 to February, 1967, they had no doubts about her
superior electoral appeal—compared to all other Congress leaders; 30
did acknowledge doubt or something stronger. Stated in other terms,
*the ratio of the élite image of Mrs. Gandhi's appeal to Indian voters
to the image of the appeal of all other Congress leaders was 2 to
1*—the ratio of Congress Parliamentary Party votes for her and for
Morarji Desai in the secret ballot on January 19, 1966.

The most striking concentration of doubt about Mrs. Gandhi's appeal lay with Indian Journalists (6 of the 9); in this respect the urban based and sophisticated communications élite was atypical —both of the élite as a whole and of the Congress MP group representing all Indian states. Only 10 of 36 MPs doubted her appeal, and of these, 4 were committed Desai supporters. By contrast with the Journalists, all 6 Opposition leaders who replied to the question agreed that Mrs. Gandhi presented the best Congress image to the electorate. So did 5 of the 6 Academics. Congress leaders, central and state, fell within the 2 to 1 ratio (10 to 4, with 2 "No Answer"). The extreme deviation of Indian Journalists in this regard is evident in the following comparison: Their image of Mrs. Gandhi's appeal relative to that of other Congress leaders is 1 to 2; the image held by the political élite as a whole is 2.5 to 1 (41 to 16 replies). *The ratio, then, in Journalists' and political élite respect for Mrs. Gandhi's appeal is 1 to 5.*

The largest group among the 23 dissenters were disenchanted at the outset—when Mrs. Gandhi was elected Prime Minister; the 8 members of the "constant negative" category were equally divided between MPs and Others, and included the two critical Cabinet Ministers. Perhaps the most striking feature of the "time of disenchantment" theme is *the minimal effect of specific acts of great controversy on the élite image of the Prime Minister of India's electoral appeal:* Only 3 persons cited the devaluation decision as the catalyst of doubt (2 were Journalists), and only 1 mentioned the Cow Riots of November, 1966. Dissent was more rooted in time.

There was only one clear alternative to Mrs. Gandhi in the élite image of electoral appeal among Congress leaders; 12 of the 23 indicated Morarji Desai, the three-time loser in the succession contests of 1964, 1966, and 1967. Others cited in this connection were Party President Kamaraj (by 2 Indian Journalists), Chavan (by 1 MP), and the deceased Prime Minister, Lal Bahadur Shastri (by 2 MPs and 1 Journalist); the 2 dissenting members of the Working Committee asserted their own superior appeal. Viewed in terms of group images of Morarji's appeal, only half of the 10 dissenting MPs thought he would have done better in the General Election; no one in the Working Committee thought so, though both dissenting

Cabinet Ministers cited Morarji; and only 2 of the 6 critical Journalists concurred. Yet despite these gaps, *Morarji emerges as the pre-eminent alternative in the élite perception of appeal with the Indian voter.*

Only three specific comments are worth noting in this context. The most intellectually oriented of the Cabinet members remarked, "Nobody else has the drawing power." But he added, "The real issue is if other decisions had been taken by another Prime Minister." One of the Journalists took a straight ideological line in his reply: "From the third week of taking power she moved to right-of-center policies." And another declared that a duumvirate between Prime Minister and Congress President would have had the maximum appeal.

TABLE 6

ELITE EXPECTATIONS ABOUT THE 1967 GENERAL
ELECTION RESULTS

Question: *Were you surprised at the extent to which the Congress Party's fortunes declined in the recent General Election?*

	Congress MPs	Others	Total
Yes	27	30	57
No	8	12	20
DUAC	1	1	2
No Answer	0	1	1

Most students of Indian politics were surprised by the results of the General Election in 1967; so too were India's élites, judged by the data in Table 6. *The over-all ratio of surprise to expectation was almost 3 to 1; it was higher among Congress MPs (3.5 to 1) and lower among Others (2.5 to 1).* A breakdown by élite groups reveals the predominance of surprise among four of them: Cabinet (5 out of 6), Working Committee (6 out of 7), Academics (5 out of 6), and Indian Journalists (8 out of 9). Approximately the same ratio obtains for the Congress rank-and-file (27 to 8) and Congress leaders (11 to 3). In short, *the incumbent political élite, university teachers, and opinion leaders shared the sense of surprise. The two deviant groups,* as might be anticipated, *were the Opposition leaders (3 of 7) and the Defeated, Disillusioned or Ex-Congressmen (1 out of 4).*

To some of those interviewed, supplementary questions were posed about their expectation regarding the number of Congress seats in the Lok Sabha, which states Congress might lose, and how many. The data have not been presented in tabular form here because they do not cover the total or even the majority of the group interviewed. Moreover, some respondents replied to one or another, but not all, of these supplementaries. Nonetheless, they may be noted here in relation to the replies of three élite groups: Of the 5 Cabinet Ministers who expressed surprise, 4 indicated that they expected 300 or more seats in the Lok Sabha, the median being 320; so too with 3 of the 5 Academics who indicated surprise; and yet, 3 of the 5 within each group added that they expected the loss of three or more states, with Kerala and Orissa mentioned by all; only 2 of the 8 Journalists elaborated on their reply.

Among the MPs only a few went beyond the "Yes" or "No" reply to the basic question. One prominent parliamentarian remarked, "It came as a cyclone." Another admitted, "I was shocked." A third said, resignedly, "It's part of democracy." And a fourth declared: "If Shastri had lived, Congress would have had a better go; also, there was too much reliance on the magic of a name." The most perceptive comment on the Congress leaders' state-of-mind came from one Working Committee member: "My travels led to an indication of impending setback, but the psychological conditioning of twenty years made it difficult to accept the indications." One Opposition leader exuded supreme confidence: "I knew the pulse of the people and expected a worse Congress defeat." Another touched the core of most MPs' image and the perception of many others: "Each man's vision is confined to his state; a regional outlook is dominant in Indian politics; thus, the Madras result did not surprise me." Among the Academics one observed, "The process of deterioration was well-built into the system." Another admitted, "I hadn't taken into account the sophistication of the electorate." One Journalist echoed the Opposition mood: "All these things were obvious to me and others." A second comment was more pointed: "Madras is a shock; no rational explanation is possible unless, as many Congressmen feel, the CIA played a big role because of Kamaraj's blunders alienating America; certainly big money was used in Madras."

As a supplementary question in this context, the élite groups were asked, *what could have been done to prevent the Congress setback?* The replies were revealing about *the thought processes of the respondents: 12 were consistent* (4 MPs and 8 Others), i.e., they either referred back to their answer from Table 2:1 or reiterated the points made earlier in the same order of importance; *17 (all but 1) MPs were inconsistent in their replies.* A few illustrations will suffice. One person *acknowledged* Internal Quarrels to be a cause in Table 2:1, but in the supplementary question he cited it as the crucial factor explaining the setback. Another did not mention Internal Quarrels or Corruption in the question of Table 2:1, but specified them as desirable preventative measures in reply to the question in Table 5. A third MP stressed Economic Problems as the most important cause of defeat and emphasized "proper leadership" in the supplementary. Perhaps the most glaring contradiction was the remark by one person, who became a Minister of State the next day, "It was too late to stop the rot"; yet in the supplementary he said, "Yes, I was surprised by the extent of defeat! "

SUMMARY AND ANALYTICAL THEMES

The principal findings of this inquiry into Indian élite images of the causes of the Congress setback at the polls may be summarized as follows:

Causes of Setback: Initiated Factors

1. A plurality of factors was ranked by the respondents, revealing sophisticated perceptions.
2. The Opposition placed greater emphasis on economic discontent than did those in power. Congress leaders were more aware of the role of Economic Problems than were the Congress rank-and-file.
3. One fourth of the political respondents mentioned Desire for Change, and almost one half of the nonpolitical respondents did so. Academics and Journalists displayed

acute perception of this intangible cause of Indian electoral behavior in 1967. Congress MPs showed considerable awareness of this mood in the electorate; and political leaders of all persuasions were hardly conscious of this factor.

4. Only Academics and the Opposition interviewees gave United Opposition a high ranking.
5. Only Congress respondents were conscious of the impact of their party's schisms on electoral behavior.
6. Congress MPs were less aware than Others of the link between quality of leadership and voters' choice. All segments of the élite perceived this factor as marginal.

Causes of Setback: Suggested Factors

7. Only 4 of 80 respondents did not regard food or prices as relevant to the election outcome.
8. Four fifths of the persons interviewed cited or acknowledged Internal Quarrels.
9. The élite as a whole attached marginal influence to special Issues.
10. In only 2 of the 6 factors—Internal Quarrels and United Opposition—is there a relatively equal frequency of initiation and responsiveness. Among the other 4 factors there is gross imbalance, heavily in favor of initiation in Economic Problems, and heavily in favor of responsiveness in special Issues, Lack of Effective Leadership, and Absence of Charismatic Leadership.
11. The élite as a whole perceived only 3 factors to be important in the General Election of 1967 — Economic Problems, Internal Quarrels, and United Opposition.

Specific Causes

12. A large proportion of respondents did not perceive any link between specific acts of the Government or Party and the election results; the governing élite was most emphatic in its denial of any connection. The only articulated exception was devaluation of the rupee in 1966 — and only the Journalists stressed its influence.

13. Government acts and Congress Party acts were perceived as synonymous by a majority of the respondents.

Charismatic Role

14. Almost half the respondents perceived charisma as a positive influence on the voters in the 1967 elections. Well over half the MPs in this group defined it as marginal. Cabinet Ministers emphasized this factor more than did Congress MPs. The difference in tone between the two segments of the Congress élite confirms the deep tension between organizational and governmental wings of the Party at the all-India level during Mrs. Gandhi's Prime Ministership.

15. Morarji Desai was the clear alternative in the élite perception of appeal to Indian voters.

Expectations About Results

16. The incumbent political élites, academics, and opinion leaders shared a sense of surprise about the results. Opposition leaders and Defeated or Ex-Congressmen did not.

Several analytic themes can be derived from these findings, but they are, of necessity, tentative. For one thing, India is almost unique among the new states of Asia and Africa in its experiment in mass democracy and mass electoral participation: Indian élite images must be analyzed within the context of a new and developing political system, with mass suffrage of unprecedented size. Secondly, the analysis of élite images is a recent innovation. Some studies have been conducted in Europe and North America, very few in the developing states. There is no body of literature which deals systematically with élite images of one's own political system. Thus no hypotheses exist to link types of élite images with the functioning of political systems. Thirdly, this study of élite images deals with one aspect of a political system, electoral behavior, not with the system as a whole. Only recently have political scientists begun to concern themselves with electoral strategy — in developed polities only. This area of inquiry into developing states has been neglected thus far.

For these reasons, the implications to be drawn from the data must be understood as preliminary work in an unexplored field.

It was noted (No. 2 above) that the two most frequently cited causes of the Congress setback were Economic Problems and the Desire for Change, that awareness of the impact of economic dislocation was greater among Opposition members, and that Congress leaders were more conscious of that factor than were Congress MPs. This relatively low level of awareness by the governing party's rank-and-file is surprising and merits comment. Most of the literature on voting behavior indicates the pre-eminence of "bread and butter" issues at the expense of "national" issues. Yet at a time of grave economic crisis in India, Congress MPs perceived Economic Problems as only one of three significant reasons for electoral revolt against Congress *Raj*.

Several explanations can be suggested for this attitude. Congress MPs are preoccupied with preserving the cohesion and power of the Congress Party; as such, they place a greater emphasis on failures of organization than on failures of economic policy. Secondly, Congressmen may be aware of the enormity of the economic difficulties faced by India; but they may see no viable alternative to Congress rule nor viable alternative economic policies. In short, Congressmen perceive economic problems as long-range in character, with little direct connection between economic dislocation and defeat at the polls.

This hypothesis is supported by Congress MPs' acute awareness of the impact of their party's internal schisms on electoral behavior, a factor underplayed by all non-Congress respondents (No. 5 above). Deficiencies in the Congress party machine, dissidence, and factionalism appear to Congress interviewees as a major factor in the election outcome. This image of the causes of the Congress setback is focused on political institutions rather than on public policy; it is essentially manipulative.

The Opposition image also offers some insights. Only 1 of 7 Opposition leaders mentioned Desire for Change as a significant cause of Congress defeat. As a group they placed much greater emphasis on Economic Problems and United Opposition than did the Congress, and they ignored internal Congress party schisms (Nos. 2-5 above). Opposition leaders, then, stressed both a manipulative factor — a United Opposition — and a grave issue of public policy — economic dislocation. As a group they are less concerned with the institutional aspects of election strategy, a logical attitude for a "permanent" opposition.

It was also noted that the Indian élite did not perceive the impact of specific policy acts on the election results (No. 12 above) in contrast to what the literature suggests. This, too, seems to underline the essentially manipulative image held by a substantial portion of the élite. Public policy in general, and specific acts of policy which may be subject to great controversy within the élite itself, are seen as irrelevant or marginal to electoral choice. Implicit is the élite view that voters respond at election-time to pre-established and long-held loyalties which have little or no connection with the content of governmental decisions.

Certain implications flow logically from this set of images. Policy-making becomes the exclusive concern of the élite. Moreover, the effect of both successful and unsuccessful policy is marginal within the political system as a whole. The gap in India is not between Congress and Opposition nor between the political and other élites; it is rather between those who engage in the policy-making process — and are aware of its results — and the masses. In short, Indian élite respondents view the vast majority of Indian voters as "subjects" — unaware of both inputs and outputs of the policy process. The emphasis placed by both Congress and Opposition respondents on institutional factors — Internal Quarrels and a United Opposition — becomes meaningful within the context of a "subject"-oriented rather than a "citizen"-oriented population.[1] Yet there is some evidence that this all-India élite image does not wholly correspond to reality. Voting studies conducted at the village and city levels in India suggest a voter awareness of policy outputs,

---

[1] G.A. Almond and S. Verba, *The Civic Culture* (Princeton, N.J: Princeton University Press, 1963). Almond and Verba postulate three types of voters: the *"subject,"* who is unaware of both inputs and outputs; the *"citizen,"* who is aware of outputs; and the *"participant,"* who is aware of both inputs and outputs. They would characterize India as "subject-participant."

that is, a "citizen" orientation. This awareness, however, is one that focuses on the relevance of policy decisions to local conditions.[2]Before any further implications can be drawn for the Indian political system, it is necessary to explore these images more deeply. If the Indian élite image is congruent with that of the voters, the making of policy and the winning of elections may be two entirely separate and unrelated tasks which the political élite of India must perform.

One further point worth noting is the rather marginal influence attributed to charisma (No.14 above). This is somewhat surprising, for the politics of development have often been described as "the politics of charisma." In the early years of the postindependence period, the giant shadow cast by the new leaders of India shaped and formed the political process. Mrs. Gandhi, as the daughter of Nehru, is the logical heir to the mantle of charisma. Yet less than one fourth of the élite respondents considered Mrs. Gandhi's charisma a helpful factor at the polls.

This is one of the many indices of the transition in Indian politics. The élite no longer sees its leadership in charismatic terms; nor does it posit charisma as a prime requisite of leadership. The evidence uncovered here seems to support an earlier conclusion that India has managed to routinize political change at the national level:[3] The political élite no longer requires a charismatic leader as a necessary condition for a relatively stable political process. We shall return to this point after exploring the Indian élite image of the qualities of a leader.

---

[2] See, for example, F.G. Bailey, *Politics and Social Changes: Orissa in 1959* (Oxford, England: Oxford University Press, 1963) and V.M. Sirsikar, *Political Behaviour in India* (Bombay: Manaktalas, 1965).

[3] Michael Brecher, "Succession in India 1967: The Routinization of Political Change," *Asian Survey*, Vol. VII, No. 7 (July, 1967), pp. 423-43 .

CHAPTER **3**

THE FOURTH GENERAL ELECTION:
· EFFECTS OF THE RESULTS

TABLE 7 : 1

ELITE ASSESSMENT OF THE EFFECTS OF THE ELECTION RESULTS

PARTY HIERARCHY vs. PARLIAMENTARY WING

Question: *Do you think the results of the Election affected the balance of power between the party hierarchy and the parliamentary wing of the Congress?*

		Congress MPs	Others	Total
Yes	No Further Reply	1	0	1
	Strengthened Party Hierarchy	7	6	13
	Strengthened Parliamentary Wing	7	8	15
	Others	2	6	8
	TOTAL	17	20	37
No	Balance of Power Unaffected	5	9	14
DUAC		3	14	17
No Answer		11	1	12

The data in Table 7:1 suggest a *blurred image of the Election impact on power relations within the Congress at the all-India level.* Amost half of the respondents perceived a change, with a slightly lesser weight among MPs than among Others; only 14 did not. Thus, there is a clear ratio of the image of change to the image of static equilibrium—2.6 to 1. Yet 29 persons or 35 per cent did not answer or did so unclearly. And among those who replied in the affirmative there was an almost equal sense of accretion of influence to the two wings of the Congress. More significantly, *there are three equally articulated images in the élite as a whole—a stronger hierarchy, a stronger parliamentary wing, and no change.*

The breakdown by groups accentuates this mélange image. Only 10 of the 16 Congress leaders gave a clear reply, a much lower proportion than for most questions: Of these, only 1 perceived a stronger hierarchy and 3, a stronger parliamentary group; but 6, 3 each from the Cabinet and the Working Committee, indicated no change. By contrast, a large majority of the Congress rank-and-file (16 to 5) did perceive a change in the power structure; the contrast is blunted, however, by the fact that they are equally divided as to who was the beneficiary; further, 11 MPs gave no answer whatever. All 4 Opposition leaders who replied saw a change, but its direction, too, is blurred. And in the case of the nonpolitical groups there is disagreement: Four of the 5 Academics affirmed a change, and 3 indicated the parliamentary wing; with Indian Journalists, the ratio is reversed. In short, there is a conspicuous lack of clarity and consensus, perhaps because, as some noted, it was too early to say. "It has not yet been realized," remarked one Academic about a shift of influence to the Parliamentary Party; "It will take eighteen months or so for this change to become recognized." Another remarked that "the situation is in flux." But a third scholar observed, "It is more the depletion of High Command strength than the accretion of influence to the CPP." One Opposition leader declared, "Both are weaker; the Parliamentary Party because of the debacle, the organization because of the defeat of Kamaraj and others." Another opined, "This is a transitional period; the tussle is on but it is not yet resolved." Among the Cabinet Ministers, two took the position that "the organizational wing must disappear"; the second of these "hard liners" asserted: "The Congress High Command is to a large extent obsolete or redundant; I feel we cannot afford two foci of power." A third urged that "the loss (of seats) by some Working Committee members does not mean the decline of the High Command." Perhaps the most telling remark came from a Congress MP: "It is considered neither High nor accepted as the Command." *Many certainly felt that, at the minimum, the CPP, long over-shadowed by the Working Committee, would be more assertive in the future.*

TABLE 7 : 2

ELITE ASSESSMENT OF THE EFFECTS OF THE ELECTION RESULTS

ON GEOGRAPHIC GROUPS WITHIN THE PARTY

Question: *Do you think the results affected the balance of power among the. geographic groups within the Party?*

		Congress MPs	Others	Total
Yes	No Further Reply	0	0	0
	New Center in Krishna-Godavari River Valley[a]	22	23	45
	Others	1	1	2
	TOTAL	23	24	47
No		13	14	27
DUAC		0	3	3
No Answer		0	3	3

[a] This includes the contiguous states of Maharashtra, Mysore, Andhra Pradesh, and Madhya Pradesh.

Viewed in the aggregate, almost 60 per cent of the respondents perceived a change in the regional balance of power within the Congress (63.5 per cent of those who gave a clear reply). Of the 47 persons in this category, all but 2 specified the area known as the Krishna-Godavari River Valley; only 2 used this term, but all named the states of Maharashtra, Mysore, Andhra Pradesh, and Madhya Pradesh; many added the contiguous state of Gujarat. In short, *the ratio of the image of change to the image of status quo in the geography of Congress power is 1.67 to 1; it is a clear but not an overwhelming image of regional redistribution of influence.*

A statistical breakdown by groups reveals differences in perception. The rank-and-file Congressmen were considerably more convinced of change (23 to 13) than the Congress leaders (7 to 6). Within the Congress leadership there is a striking difference: Only 2

of the 6 Cabinet Ministers perceived a change, while 5 of the 6
members of the Working Committee did so. *If one compares the
political and nonpolitical élites as a whole, there is a sharp contrast* in
the image of change to that of status quo in the loci of influence
within the leading party: *For the former it is 1.5 to 1, for the latter,
3 to 1. The politicians were less willing or less able to recognize this
impact of the election results.* Most pronounced among those who did
perceive change were Indian Journalists (7 to 2); the least were
Cabinet Ministers (2 of 6). Very few gave unclear or no replies: Of
the 6, all but 1 were political leaders, 3 each from the Congress and
the Opposition; no MP faltered on this question. The distribution of
response by geographic area is noteworthy: Eight of the 22 MP
respondents who indicated a shift in influence to the Krishna-
Godavari River Valley represented constituencies within that region,
5 came from the "Hindi Heartland," and 9 from other parts of India.
Of the 13 who perceived no change in this respect, 2 were from the
Krishna-Godavari River Valley, 4 were from Hindi-speaking states,
and 7 from other parts of India.

One Indian Journalist took the straightforward position,
"Wherever the Congress lost in the elections, the influence of those
states in the Congress declined." Another dissented, claiming that
"there is not a one-one correlation." A third termed the shift of the
Congress "heartland" from UP-Bihar or the Gangetic Plain to the
Krishna-Godavari River Valley as "accidental and transitory";
indeed, many perceived the UP as a continuing geographic center of
the Congress. Still another commentator observed that much of the
rimland — south and east coast — and almost all the border states
have been lost by the Congress. Among the Academics, one remarked, "The election results produced conditions making for a
shift, even if the shift has not fully taken place." Another suggested
that the change in locus of Congress power has been in personalities
not in geography. ("Dinesh Singh has moved to the center of
power.") And a third expressed total dissent: "What has happened
are local phenomena, which are then added up. Is it methodologically
sound? " Perhaps the most confused and confusing remark among
those who saw a change came from a Working Committee member:
"The South was a balancing factor, along with Bengal and Orissa;

now, with the loss of Madras the non-Hindi area has lost part of its influence; but the Hindi area is weaker too; the Krishna-Godavari area is safest — but not so safe either; even Madhya Pradesh is not so strong."

TABLE 7 : 3

ELITE ASSESSMENT OF THE EFFECTS OF THE ELECTION RESULTS

WORKING COMMITTEE vs. STATE CHIEF MINISTERS

Question: *Did the results affect the balance of power between the Working Committee and the State Chief Ministers?*

		Congress MPs	Others	Total
Yes	No Further Reply	0	0	0
	Chief Ministers Stronger	14	18	32
	Working Committee Stronger	5	4	9
	Others	2	8	10
	TOTAL	21	30	51
No		10	9	19
DUAC		4	4	8
No Answer		1	1	2

There is *a clear trend in favor of the proposition that the balance of power had changed between the Working Committee and the State Chief Ministers:* Fifty-one of the 80 respondents so contended; and of those who replied, the proportion is very high (51 of 70, or 73 per cent); only 19 perceived that no change had occurred as a result of the elections. *The ratio* for the composite élite groups *is,* then, *2.7 to 1 in favor of the image of change. There is also a clear trend as to the direction of change:* Thirty-two opted for the Chief Ministers, 9 for the Working Committee, *a ratio of 3.5 to 1.*

Among the separate élite groups, Indian Journalists and Academics exhibited the sharpest image of change, 9 out of 9 and 5 out of 6, respectively. This was closely followed by Opposition leaders, 5 out of 7. Congress MPs showed a slight majority in this view, 21 of the 36, while the Cabinet, Working Committee, and Chief Ministers were each equally divided between the perception of change and of the status quo. *The communications and educational élites had a much sharper perception of change in the balance of power than did the composite image of the political élites.* Indeed, the contrast is extreme — *14 to 1 versus 2.7 to 1; the political respondents were much more hesitant about analyzing election consequences.*

No less striking is the evidence of group perceptions *within* the image of change category. Again, Indian Journalists and Academics stand out: Seven out of 8, and 4 out of 5, respectively, perceived a strengthening of the Chief Ministers. The rank-and-file Congressmen shared this image by almost 3 to 1 (14 out of 19), as did the Working Committee; the Cabinet image was less clear, 2 out of 3. At the other extreme were Opposition leaders — 4 out of 5 indicated "Others" as the beneficiaries of the elections. In short, *the nonpolitical élites were overwhelmingly convinced that the Chief Ministers emerged stronger; the Opposition claimed that neither Working Committee nor state leaders benefited; and no group perceived the Working Committee as stronger.*

Respondents espousing the status quo view were widely represented; there were no peaks in the distribution, but no one among the nonpolitical interviewees shared this image. A higher proportion than that in response to the preceding question fell in the "DUAC" or "No Answer" categories, 10 out of 80 compared to 6 out of 80.

Many respondents elaborated on their initial "Yes" or "No" reply, but few comments contained any substance. One Journalist perceived that the influence of Congress Chief Ministers had declined because of the presence of a majority of non-Congress Chief Ministers as a counterweight in center-state decision-making. A senior Cabinet Minister concurred, adding, "It will bring more sobriety to the Congress Chief Ministers." Another Journalist noted that the relationship between Working Committee members and Chief Ministers "was always vague, because the Chief Ministers sit in the Working Committee." And one Academic reflected the blurred image of some respondents: "These things have still to be worked out."

TABLE 7 : 4

ELITE ASSESSMENT OF THE EFFECTS OF THE ELECTION RESULTS ON THE POWER POSITION OF THE CONGRESS PRESIDENT

Question: *What effects do you think the election results have had on the position of the Congress President relative to the following ... ?*

	Congress MPs	Others	Total
Working Committee			
Stronger	0	0	0
Weaker	22	26	48
Unchanged	11	8	19
DUAC	2	9	11
No Answer	1	1	2
Congress Parliamentary Party			
Stronger	0	0	0
Weaker	23	27	50
Unchanged	9	7	16
DUAC	3	9	12
No Answer	1	1	2
State Chief Ministers			
Stronger	1	0	1
Weaker	20	27	47
Unchanged	11	7	18
DUAC	2	9	11
No Answer	2	1	3
Mrs. Gandhi			
Stronger	0	0	0
Weaker	22	27	49
Unchanged	10	9	19
DUAC	3	7	10
No Answer	1	1	2
Morarji Desai			
Stronger	4	7	11
Weaker	17	19	36
Unchanged	11	8	19
DUAC	3	9	12
No Answer	1	1	2

(Continued)

TABLE 7 : 4 — *Continued*

	Congress MPs	Others	Total
Y.B. Chavan			
Stronger	1	0	1
Weaker	18	19	37
Unchanged	11	12	23
DUAC	4	11	15
No Answer	2	2	4

The position of the Congress President has been weakened across the whole spectrum of institutions and persons in the Congress power élite — this is the pre-eminent strand in the composite image of the Election's impact in this sphere. Not a single respondent perceived a *stronger* position for the Party President vis-à-vis the Working Committee, the Congress Parliamentary Party (CPP), or the Prime Minister, Mrs. Gandhi; and only 1 person indicated greater influence with the Chief Ministers or closer relations with Home Minister Chavan. *The only (partial) deviation from this consensus focused on the Kamaraj-Morarji Desai relationship:* Eleven of 80 persons perceived it to be stronger.

More pointed was the frequency of an articulated image of a *weaker* position for the Congress President: About 60 per cent of the total respondents fell in this category (more than 70 per cent of those who gave a clear reply) regarding his relationship with the Working Committee, CPP, Chief Ministers, and the Prime Minister. With respect to the Deputy Prime Minister and the Home Minister, the proportion declined to 45 per cent of the total respondents (54 and 60 per cent respectively, of those who gave a clear reply).

There is also a substantial group of respondents, ranging from 20 to 25 per cent of the total, even higher with regard to Home Minister Chavan, who perceived *no change* in the Congress President's position of influence within institutions or friendship with persons. *The ratios of the composite élite image of a weaker position of the Congress President to the image of no change are as follows:*

2.5 to 1 re the Working Committee   2.6 to 1 re Mrs. Gandhi (PM)
3.1 to 1 re the CPP   1.9 to 1 re Morarji Desai (Deputy PM)
2.6 to 1 re the Chief Ministers   1.6 to 1 re Chavan (Home Minister)

Elite images of the first four relationships in Table 7: 4 may be analyzed together because the statistical breakdown by groups within each of the two categories, "weaker" and "unchanged," is almost identical. Thus, 20 to 23 of the 36 Congress MPs indicated a weaker position for the Congress President; 26 to 27 of the 44 Others concurred. The number of MPs who perceived no change ranged from 9 to 11, Others, from 7 to 9. Among Congress leaders the ratio of the image of "weaker" to the image of "unchanged" averaged 9 to 5; but within that group of respondents there is a conspicuous difference in the image held by the Cabinet and the Working Committee. Only 2 or 3 of the 6 Ministers perceived a weaker position, but Working Committee interviewees were emphatic in indicating greater weakness (5 of 7 re the Working Committee, CPP, and PM, and 6 of 7 re the Chief Ministers).

The three other major groups of respondents agreed with the Working Committee members — even more emphatically: All 7 Opposition leaders indicated a greater weakness for the Congress President in the four relationships; among the Academics, all who replied (4 or 5 in different categories) took the same position, except for 1 person who perceived an unchanged relationship with the Chief Ministers and the PM; so too with all the Indian Journalists who replied (4 or 5 in different categories), except for the one choice of "unchanged" regarding his relationship to the Working Committee.

The 11 respondents who perceived a stronger relationship between Kamaraj and Morarji Desai were distributed among five groups. There was a heavier weight among Others (7) than among Congress MPs (4). Only 2 Congress leaders, both Working Committee members, fell in this group; 3 of the 6 Journalists concurred. Yet, even with this deviation almost half the rank-and-file Congressmen (17 of the 36), half the Congress leaders (7 of the 14), half the Academics (3 of the 6), and almost all Opposition leaders (6 of the 7) perceived a weaker relationship as a result of the 1967 Election.

A very similar distribution obtains in the image of the Congress President's relationship with Home Minister Chavan, with two exceptions: Only 1 person perceived a closer relationship, compared to· 11 re Morarji Desai; and the 10 are distributed mainly in the "unchanged" and "DUAC" categories. The conclusion from this wealth of evidence is unmistakable: *Congress President Kamaraj emerged from the Elections with sharply diminished authority and influence, in the consensus image of India's élites.*

The comments of those who perceived a general weakening of the Congress President's position ranged along a wide spectrum. At one extreme — with the notion of minimal change — was a Journalist's remark that other party leaders "would feel a greater permissiveness to criticize him"; few shared this image. Another noted that he had been weakened "as an individual and as an institution." And at the other extreme were those who noted that he had lost his indispensable political base; some unkindly asserted that "he had become a stateless person." A widely shared perception was that he retained far greater influence than could be objectively expected; this was displayed in the third succession struggle over the Prime Ministership, an occasion for surprise among participants and observers alike; and this role, according to some interviewees, enabled Kamaraj to recoup his position in part. Yet, as in the preceding cases, the "kingmaker's" influence declined by half after the coronation; and, in 1967, his initial base and quantity of influence were slender; there were few sources to sustain it.

TABLE 8

ELITE ASSESSMENT OF THE EFFECTS OF THE ELECTION RESULTS
ON CANDIDATES FOR THE PRIME MINISTERSHIP

Question: *Do you think the election results benefited any candidate for the Prime Ministership?*
(To those who replied "yes," the further question, "who" was posed.)

		Congress MPs	Others	Total
Yes	No Further Reply	0	0	0
	Mrs. Gandhi	13	21	34
	Morarji Desai	3	2	5
	Others	1	2	3
	TOTAL	17	25	42
No		15	16	31
DUAC		3	2	5
No Answer		1	1	2

The data in Table 8 reveal that slightly more than half the total number of respondents perceived some electoral benefit to a candidate for the Prime Ministership; the proportion rises to almost 58 per cent of clear replies. More significantly, *80 per cent of the persons who perceived some electoral effect on the succession contest identified Mrs. Gandhi as the beneficiary;* only 12 per cent, 5 persons, indicated Morarji Desai in this respect. *Within the crucial Congress MP group* — which would have cast the ballots in an election of the CPP Leader — *the ratio of its image of electoral benefit to Mrs. Gandhi to that in favor of Morarji Desai was 4.3 to 1; among Others it was* an astounding *10.5 to 1.*

Not surprisingly, relatively fewer rank-and-file Congressmen perceived this effect of the General Election than did Others — 36 to 48 per cent. Congress leaders were much more convinced of this electoral legacy (8 of the 9, or almost 90 per cent of those who perceived a benefit — and not 1 for Morarji). Further down the scale of perception on this aspect were Academics (3 out of 4), Indian Journalists (4 out of 6), and, at the other extreme, Opposition leaders (2 out of 6). In short, *Congress leaders were most aware of this link, the Opposition, least aware, with Congress MPs only a shade more sensitive.* If one takes the political and nonpolitical élites as a whole, the composite image of the former, that Mrs. Gandhi was the beneficiary of the election results, was 26 to 3 or 8.7 to 1; for the latter it was 7 to 2, or 3.5 to 1. Indeed, not a single member of the political élite other than MPs perceived Morarji as the beneficiary.

The Congress rank-and-file was, on the whole, reticent about this link; in fact, fewer acknowledged a benefit to one of the candidates than did not (13 to 15); in the case of Others the sensitivity to election results as a component of the third succession was greater (21 to 16). The only groups where a significant proportion did not perceive this connection were, apart from MPs, Opposition leaders (4 out of 6) and Journalists (3 out of 9). Viewed in aggregate group terms, the nonpolitical élite perceived an electoral benefit by 11 to 6, whereas the political élite did so by a slender majority, 31 to 25; *the difference in perception was almost 2 to 1. Most important, Mrs. Gandhi was the overwhelming choice of beneficiary in the aggregate image.*

Four reasons were given by Congress MPs who perceived a benefit to Mrs. Gandhi's candidacy. Some key party leaders, notably the Syndicate, who had opposed her or had been unenthusiastic, were defeated at the polls. Secondly, the UP, on whose votes Morarji's camp depended a great deal, saw a serious decline in Congress strength. Thirdly, and most important, the four crucial states of the Krishna-Godavari River Valley, where Congress did well — Maharashtra, Mysore, Andhra Pradesh, and Madhya Pradesh — were led by Chief Ministers strongly supporting Mrs. Gandhi. And finally, as an MP remarked, "The debacle created pressure for the status quo." The Cabinet Ministers concurred with the first and third reason; one member of the Cabinet added another — the Prime Minister's power of patronage. A Working Committee member suggested still another reason — the diminished influence of Kamaraj to shape the succession contest because of the Madras disaster; Kamaraj was known to be less opposed now to Morarji Desai than in the first two successions. A few Academics echoed the point about the Krishna-Godavari political bastion; one of them suggested another reason — "The rise to power of non-Congress ministries in Madras, Kerala, and elsewhere helped her candidacy, for a Prime Minister was needed who could co-exist with them." One Journalist stated this reason as well. Another contended that many successful Congress candidates for the Lok Sabha had been financed by a few business houses, and they had indicated their support for Mrs. Gandhi. And finally, one commentator observed, "Morarji created a certain allergy in the South." *The aggregate analysis on this question was impressive for its range of persuasive explanation of the link between election results and succession contest.*

Among those who perceived Morarji Desai to be the beneficiary, the most imaginative view came from one Academic: "The results showed that Mrs. Gandhi was not a vote-catcher"; it also showed that her tenure as PM had been unsuccessful, and it knocked out her Madras base. "But for these three reasons Morarji would not be Deputy Prime Minister, and but for his ineptness he could have been Prime Minister."

TABLE 9 : 1

ATTITUDE TO THE PRIME MINISTER BEFORE THE 1967 GENERAL ELECTION

Question: *Did you at any time during the year of Mrs. Gandhi's Prime Minister-ship think that it might be desirable to have a change of Prime Minister after the General Election?*

(To those who answered, "yes," the further questions, "when" and "why" were posed.)

	Congress MPs	Others	Total
Yes	9	22	31
No	24	21	45
DUAC	1	0	1
No Answer	2	1	3
Yes			
At Outset	4	7	11
At Devaluation	1	4	5
At Cow Riots	0	2	2
Others and DUAC	3	2	5
No Answer	1	7	8
Yes			
Post Too Demanding	1	1	2
Weak Leadership	2	1	3
Others and DUAC	3	11	14
No Answer	3	9	12

It is noteworthy that *a clear majority of the total respondents* (45 out of 80, or more precisely 45 out of 76) *recalled complete satisfaction with Mrs. Gandhi's leadership during her first year in office;* less than 40 per cent thought a change in the Prime Ministership might be desirable. *The weightage in the contemplation of change category is overwhelmingly with Others, 70 per cent;* among the satisfied there is a slight majority of MPs, 24 to 21. More significant, however, in terms of the selection process for the Prime Minister, is the breakdown of preference by groups of respondents.

Only 25 per cent of the Congress MPs gave thought in 1966 or early 1967, to the desirability of a change in the Head of

Government; two thirds did not. Among the Others, by contrast, more favored a change than did not, a shade more than 50 per cent. In short, *the ratio of the proportion of Others who contemplated a change in leadership to the proportion of MPs who did so was 2 to 1.* In terms of the selection of a Prime Minister, the more pertinent relationship lies *within the MP group:* Nine thought a change desirable, 24 did not, *a ratio of .375 to 1.* Congress leaders were even more emphatic than the rank-and-file in their preference — 12 to 3 *against* a change, with 2 of the dissenters in the Working Committee; the Academics' attitude was similar to that of MPs, 4 to 2 *against* a change. *The one noteworthy deviation from this pattern was the communications élite:* Seven of the 9 Indian Journalists were dissatisfied with Mrs. Gandhi's leadership in 1966. As might be expected, Opposition leaders and the Defeated or Ex-Congressmen felt the same way.

Among the 31 persons who questioned the quality of Mrs. Gandhi's leadership at some point in 1966, 11, or slightly more than a third, were critical from the outset; these included 4 of the 9 MPs, the 1 Cabinet Minister who wanted a change, but only a small proportion of the dissatisfied Academics and Journalists, 3 out of 9. The devaluation decision added 5 persons to the disenchanted and the Cow Riots, 2 others. Thus, *dissatisfaction with Mrs. Gandhi's leadership stemmed from general and more long-term sources; specific decisions or acts in 1966 exerted only marginal influence.*

The most revealing facet of the data in the third part of Table 9:1 is the *paucity of specific articulated reasons for disenchantment.* Only 5 out of 31 persons indicated a precise factor explaining their contemplation of change in leadership; 12 did not elaborate at all.

There were only three elaborative comments by MPs on this question — and all were atypical of the aggregate élite attitudes. One saw no need for individual choice in this matter: "I never thought of this question; I have supreme faith in the Organization." Another confessed astonishment: "I did not apply my mind to this question." And a third expressed the opinion that "the Prime Minister's office is not so important after Panditji's death." One of the Opposition leaders observed, "From the country's viewpoint, Morarji would be a better PM; from the Opposition viewpoint, Mrs. Gandhi would be better." Another remarked that he naturally preferred a non-Congress PM but did not see this as feasible prior to the 1967 elections; now he predicted a change within fifteen months. Two of the Journalists criticized Mrs. Gandhi's entourage. "She has a tendency to rely on people who were moved by petty motives," said one. "The control of the levers of power rests with a small group of advisers," declared the other. A Cabinet Minister who contemplated a change concurred. And one Academic cited the "soft line" in negotiations with the Nagas, as well as the Cow Riots of November, 1966 to indicate Government weakness: "The picture of Government insecurity created a sense of anxiety in my mind."

TABLE 9 : 2

EFFECT OF THE ELECTION RESULTS ON ATTITUDE TO CHANGE OF LEADERSHIP

Question: *Did the election results make you feel that a change of leadership is desirable?*

	Congress MPs	Others	Total
Yes	7	14	21
No	23	26	49
DUAC	2	2	4
No Answer	4	2	6

Despite the Congress debacle at the polls, the desire for change in leadership declined considerably — from 31 to 21 respondents, or from 40 to 30 per cent of actual replies. Ironically, it would seem, *Mrs Gandhi's position improved as a result of the election setback.* The disenchanted among the rank-and-file remained almost unchanged — a shift from 9 to 7 MPs. But a noticeable decline in criticism of Mrs. Gandhi's leadership is evident in Others — from 22 to 14 or almost 40 per cent.

The basic change in attitude is centered in the two nonpolitical élite groups: Both Academics, a decline from 2 to 0, and Indian

Journalists, a decline of 7 to 3, did not perceive the election results as requiring a change in the Prime Ministership. If one excludes Opposition leaders and Defeated or Ex-Congressmen, natural loci of dissent, *the respondents who did feel the need for a change* after the Elections of 1967 *were concentrated in three groups* – MPs (7), *Working Committee* (3), and *Indian Journalists* (3).

The number of MPs who remained loyal to Mrs. Gandhi was almost constant (24 to 23). Others increased by 5 (from 21 to 26 – 1 Academic and 4 Journalists). In short, *the election results affected the attitude of nonpolitical élite members to Mrs. Gandhi's leadership much more than it did political interviewees – and the impact was to solidify her claim to the succession.* The other notable change in élite response was the increase of "DUAC" or "No Answer" replies from 4 to 10, double among MPs, four times among Others. *In summary,* the attitude of rank-and-file Congressmen to Mrs. Gandhi as PM remained unaffected by the election setbacks – as it had been by specific stimuli (acts or decisions) during the turbulent year, 1966. By contrast, Others, notably university professors and opinion leaders were acutely sensitive to the verdict at the polls, many interpreting it as a call for new leadership.

The view of MPs who were loyal in the face of an election debacle was summed up by one respondent with the words, "It was no fault of hers." Among the critics, the major theme was that "she is no substitute for her father or Shastri." The sole antifeminist attitude among the 80 respondents was expressed by another MP: "Politics is no place for a woman, especially as a leader." One Journalist expressed his acquiescence in Mrs. Gandhi's continuation as Prime Minister: "I would have been happy had there been a charismatic figure with a modern, administrative outlook." Another said, resignedly, "The choice was only between two persons – and I wouldn't have chosen either." But a third remarked, "Mrs. Gandhi represents the greatest common denominator." An Academic spoke for some when he said, "The difficulty was – there was no alternative." A Cabinet Minister concurred; he did not object to a change, "but I found it was not possible." Another reflected a growing view during the succession struggle: "The election results highlighted for me the importance of Indira and Morarji working together."

SUMMARY AND ANALYTICAL THEMES

Effects on Congress

1. There is a conspicuous lack of consensus in the élite perception of the Election impact on power relations within the Party at the all-India level. Three images were articulated with equal support — a stronger hierarchy, a stronger parliamentary wing, and no change.
2. Almost 60 per cent of the respondents perceived a change in the regional balance of power within the Congress, in favor of the Krishna- Godavari River Valley. Political interviewees, especially the Cabinet Ministers, were less willing or less able to recognize this impact on the election outcome.
3. There is a striking image that the balance of influence within the Congress moved from the Working Committee to the State Chief Ministers. The nonpolitical respondents were overwhelmingly convinced of this change. Opposition leaders asserted that neither wing of the Congress benefited from the 1967 elections. No group perceived the Working Committee as stronger.
4. There was widespread agreement that the position of the Congress President had been weakened in relation to institutions and persons within the Party élite. The only partial exception in this consensus related to the Kamaraj-Morarji Desai relationship. This image of the Congress President's diminished authority and influence is more pronounced among Congress MPs than among the Party's leaders.

Effects on Contest for Prime Ministership

5. Slightly more than half the respondents perceived an effect of the election outcome on the succession contest; of those who did so, four fifths identified Mrs. Gandhi as the

beneficiary. Congress leaders were most sensitive to this link, the Opposition least aware, and Congress MPs only slightly more aware than the latter.

6. A slight majority of the respondents recalled complete satisfaction with Mrs. Gandhi's leadership during her first year as the Head of Government. Only one fourth of the Congress MP interviewees favored a change, and only one fifth of the Congress leaders did so. Whatever dissatisfaction existed was due to general, not specific, factors.

7. The Congress setback at the polls led to a decline in the desire for change in Prime Minister — Mrs. Gandhi's claim to continuance in office appeared to be strengthened. The attitude of Congress MPs to the leadership issue was relatively unaffected by the election results, that of Working Committee members more so, and the nonpolitical respondents were influenced most of all.

The Congress was the most important political institution in India during the first twenty years of independence. The party underwent several phases of development and change, but it maintained a near-monopoly of power until 1967. It was the Fourth General Election that first seriously altered the delicate balance among various segments within that omnibus organization.

Perhaps the most immediate effect was a shift in the regional balance of influence within the party. As noted (No. 2 above), almost 60 per cent of the élite respondents perceived a geographic change in favor of the Krishna-Godavari River Valley, comprising the four contiguous states of Maharashtra, Madhya Pradesh, Mysore, and Andhra Pradesh. The unwillingness or inability of Congress leaders to acknowledge this regional shift may be due partly to the heavy representation of the "Hindi Heartland" of UP and Bihar in the federal Cabinet. Congress MPs were much more aware of the implications of the Congress setback in those states and were more willing to recognize a change in the authority structures within their party.

It should be re-emphasized at this point that the survey questions were consciously phrased from an all-India perspective.

The writer does not deny the importance of regional variations and the necessity for a regional framework in explaining both the defeat of several Congress state governments and the drastically reduced Congress representation in Parliament. The aim of this study, however, is to illuminate the images of *all-India élites* and thereby to fill a glaring gap in the literature of Indian politics. In this context, Congress MPs revealed a more flexible all-India perspective. They were quicker to perceive changes in regional influence than were their leaders, who had a more fixed image of the sources of Congress' strength. Moreover, the Congress rank-and-file were more attuned to the scope and impact of regional variations, both on the institutional machinery of the party and on federal politics. One would have expected the reverse.

Congress leaders and MPs, as noted (No. 3 above), were divided on the implications of the election results for the balance of power between the Working Committee and State Chief Ministers. If the Congress rank-and-file had been consistent, they would have perceived greater influence for the state leaders; they did not do so. Their understanding of the impact of regional variations on Congress stopped short of predicting a fundamental change in the locus of decision-making within the party. In short, their image of the effect of regional shifts was confined to all-India *institutional machinery.*

This hypothesis is supported by the acute rank-and-file image of the Congress Presidency. That office has become one of the key centers of decision-making within the party in recent years. In particular, the President played this crucial role during the three succession contests of the post-Nehru era (1964, 1966, 1967). Congress MPs were much more explicit in their image of the President's postelection weakness than were Congress leaders, though this perception was widely shared by all sections of the élite (No. 4 above). Moreover, this perception is inextricably tied to two events in the 1967 elections: Kamaraj lost his parliamentary seat and the Congress Party was badly defeated in Madras, the Congress President's home state. It is possible that élite respondents so completely identified the office of the Presidency with Kamaraj that the widely held image of increased weakness is a product of the electoral defeats suffered by Kamaraj. Nevertheless, the Congress rank-and-file were more aware than their leaders of changes in the relative power of the Presidency. In this sphere, too, Congress MPs articulated a more flexible image of institutional patterns and were quicker to detect possible shifts in long-term relationships between the head of the party and its membership.

The nonpolitical respondents as a group were overwhelmingly convinced of substantial changes in the pattern of Congress influence. They emphasized both the increased strength of the Chief Ministers and the increased weakness of the Congress Presidency. All segments of the élite agreed that the Working Committee had not emerged stronger. Paradoxically, then, Congress leaders were least aware of the shifts and nuances produced by the 1967 election results. They were best-equipped of all élite groups to formulate a sensitive and flexible all-India response, yet their image was the most static and brittle. The Congress rank-and-file are parochial by background, interests, and their local-regional basis of selection. Yet their image was more dynamic and more attuned to actual and potential shifts in power. The communications élite, as expected, demonstrated the sharpest image of the election effects on the Congress Party.

It was also noted (No. 5 above) that 80 per cent of the respondents who perceived some electoral effect on the succession contest identified Mrs. Gandhi as the beneficiary; nonpolitical respondents were definite in this assessment. Congress leaders were the most aware of this link and were convinced of the electoral benefits to the incumbent Prime Minister. In this delicate area of all-India politics, Congress leaders had the most sophisticated and most finely tuned image among the élite respondents, probably because many of them were involved directly or peripherally in the two preceding succession contests.

Congress leaders were also the most emphatic in their desire to retain Mrs. Gandhi as Prime Minister. A large majority of MPs, too, expressed satisfaction with her leadership. And it was extremely difficult for those who were dissatisfied (Journalists and Opposition leaders) to articulate specific reasons for their disenchantment (No. 6 above). One may suggest, then, that both specific policy acts and the Congress setback at the polls had little influence on the succession contest; even within the élite there is a strong tendency to de-emphasize the relevance of policy. As stated in another context, the success or failure of policy is of marginal influence on élite attitudes toward the leadership issue. The available evidence supports this hypothesis. In fact, the Congress election debacle seems to have reduced the desire for change at the summit among political élite respondents.

There are two possible explanations for this phenomenon. The Congress élite undoubtedly attempted to consolidate its ranks when faced with major electoral defeat. This is not entirely satisfactory, however, for it is not consonant with the indifference to specific policy acts of Mrs. Gandhi. More plausible is the thesis that élite attitudes toward their leaders are a microcosm of their general image of the Indian electorate as a whole; the élite conviction that policy-making and policy outcomes, a large segment of political life, are irrelevant to the electoral process has spilled over into their own selection of leaders. If this is so, choices are based on a more diffuse image, unrelated to specific decisions and policy content. The following chapter on the qualities expected of an Indian Prime Minister in 1967 will further explore this hypothesis.

CHAPTER **4**

QUALITIES OF LEADERSHIP:
ASSESSMENT OF CONGRESS CANDIDATES

TABLE 10

ELITE VIEW OF THE REQUISITE QUALITIES FOR PRIME MINISTER OF INDIA (SPRING, 1967)

RESPONDENT INITIATED QUALITIES

Question: *If you were given complete authority by the President to select a Prime Minister for India, what would you regard as the most important qualities for this post in the context of the current state of affairs?*

	Congress MPs	Others	Total
National Image			
Priority 1	0	1	1
2	2	2	4
3	3	0	3
4	3	0	3
5-8	1	1	2
International Image			
Priority 1	1	0	1
2	0	0	0
3	0	0	0
4	0	1	1
5-8	3	1	4
Holding Congress Together			
Priority 1	2	4	6
2	5	1	6
3	3	1	4
4	1	1	2
5-8	0	2	2
Maintaining North-South Unity			
Priority 1	4	2	6
2	2	3	5
3	1	1	2
4	2	0	2
5-8	0	1	1
Satisfactory to Minorities			
Priority 1	0	0	0
2	0	0	0
3	0	2	2
4	0	0	0
5-8	0	1	1

(Continued)

TABLE 10 — *Continued*

	Congress MPs	Others	Total
Effective Leadership			
Priority 1	3	3	6
2	7	4	11
3	2	2	4
4	0	4	4
5-8	4	3	7
Strong Leader			
Priority 1	4	2	6
2	1	4	5
3	3	2	5
4	3	1	4
5-8	4	4	8
Flexible Leader			
Priority 1	0	1	1
2	1	0	1
3	2	4	6
4	1	1	2
5-8	0	0	0
Ability To Deal With Opposition in Parliament			
Priority 1	0	0	0
2	1	1	2
3	0	0	0
4	0	2	2
5-8	0	0	0
Ability To Deal With States			
Priority 1	3	1	4
2	0	2	2
3	1	3	4
4	1	0	1
5-8	0	2	2
Harmony With Party Leaders			
Priority 1	0	1	1
2	1	1	2
3	2	1	3
4	1	1	2
5-8	3	2	5

	Congress MPs	Others	Total
Implementation of Socialist Program			
Priority 1	0	1	1
2	0	0	0
3	0	1	1
4	0	0	0
5-8	1	0	1
Ability To Solve Economic Problems			
Priority 1	0	2	2
2	0	4	4
3	1	2	3
4	2	4	6
5-8	2	2	4
Providing A Better Climate For Business	NONE		
Pursuing A Successful Foreign Policy	NONE		
Others			
Priority 1	18	20	38
2	14	14	28
3	9	11	20
4	8	9	17
5-8	6	10	16
No Entry For Priority			
Priority 1	1	6	7
2	3	7	10
3	9	14	23
4	14	20	34
5	22	28	50

Note: The 15 specific qualities noted in this table were used in the question for Table 11. These qualities were not mentioned to the interviewees in posing the question for Table 10.

Where appropriate, the replies to this question were classified among the 15 qualities later used as the basis for ranking Congress leaders in terms of suitability for the Prime Ministership. These 15 qualities were not divulged to the respondents at this point; they were merely categories to order the data. And no limits or restrictions were imposed on the interviewees regarding the number, the wording, or the substance of the qualities they could initiate. The results may be analyzed on two levels — aggregate and group analysis.

Aggregate Analysis

Among the 15 base qualities later employed for leadership ranking, only 6 were cited more than once as Priority 1 in the *initiating* replies of the 80 persons interviewed. An even larger number of other, unstructured qualities (8) were introduced by the respondents, each at least twice. The order of frequency in the aggregate as Priority 1 quality was as follows:

Effective Leadership [a]	6
Strong Leadership [a]	6
Holding Congress Together	6
Maintaining North-South Unity	6
National Outlook [b]	5
Boldness, Courage, Dynamism [b]	5
Intellectual Distinction [b]	5
Ability to Deal with States	4
Mass Contact (or Support) [b]	4
Integrity [b]	3
Inspiration to People [b]	3

[a] These 2 are essentially the same and may be combined to indicate a frequency of 12 for the quality of Effectiveness.

[b] These qualities are not among the 15 base qualities of ranking.

Qualities mentioned as Priority 1 by 2 persons were Ability to Solve Economic Problems, Modern, Liberal Outlook, and Patriotism. There was also a host of qualities mentioned as Priority 1 by one person: Among the 15 base qualities, as set out in Table 10, these comprised National Image, International Image, Flexibility, Harmony with Party (Congress) Leaders, and the Implementation of a Socialist Program. An even wider spectrum is evident among other qualities cited by one person: Honesty, Firmness, Restoration of *Swadeshi* Spirit, Empathy for Indian Spirit, Pragmatism, Adherence to Congress Ideals, Acumen, Adherence to Nehru's policies, and Building a Team. Thus Priority 1 in leadership was given by the 73 actual replies to no less than 30 qualities — 13 of the 15 base qualities and 17 others. In short, there was *a remarkable diversity in the élite choice of the most important quality required for India's Prime Minister in 1967.* This *pluralist character of élite attitudes to leadership qualities* is also reflected along the scale of priorities.

In terms of *Priority 2*, only 6 of the 15 base qualities were mentioned more than twice. Three other qualities were also cited by more than 2 persons. In order of frequency, they are: Effective Leadership (11), Holding Congress Together (6), Strong Leadership and Maintaining North-South Unity (5 each), National Image and Ability to Solve Economic Problems (4 each); among the other qualities, Integrity (4), and Honesty and Mass Contact (3 each). The only changes among the 6 base qualities from Priority 1 to 2 were the addition of National Image and the deletion of Ability to Deal with the States; the most notable change among other qualities was the addition of Honesty. As further evidence of pluralism, 4 other base qualities were cited in Priority 2, as were 12 other qualities — 5 of them twice and 7 once.

If one uses a simple frequency count as the basis for ranking initiated qualities, the results are as follows — for qualities with a frequency of 10 and above:

Effective Leadership	32 (16 MPs, 16 Others)
Strong Leadership	28 (15 MPs, 13 Others)
Holding Congress Together	20 (11 MPs, 9 Others)
Ability to Solve Economic Problems	19 (5 MPs, 14 Others)
Maintaining North-South Unity	16 (9 MPs, 7 Others)
Integrity [a]	15 (8 MPs, 7 Others)
Ability to Deal With States	13 (5 MPs, 8 Others)
National Image	13 (9 MPs, 4 Others)
Harmony With Party Leaders	13 (7 MPs, 6 Others)
Flexibility	10 (4 MPs, 6 Others)
Mass Contact [a]	10 (5 MPs, 5 Others)
Intellectual Distinction [a]	10 (5 MPs, 5 Others)
Inspiration to People [a]	10 (6 MPs, 4 Others)

[a]These qualities are not among the 15 base qualities.

Noteworthy is the absence of a single reference to Pursuing a Successful Foreign Policy. *In 1967, not one member of a composite élite of 80 Indians considered foreign policy of sufficient importance to indicate skill in this sphere of public policy as necessary to a Prime Minister of India in the context of current affairs – in any of the 8 priorities of leadership qualities.* The other quality mentioned by none was Providing a Better Climate for Business, indicating a consensus in the élite as a whole that private enterprise occupies, at most, a marginal role in India's economic growth.

Group Analysis

The articulated attitude of *Congress MPs* reveals *inventiveness and pluralism in the choice of leadership qualities.* All but 5 indicated qualities that fell within the 15 base categories, as well as others. The qualities initiated by 4 MPs were confined to the base categories, while 1 MP was unwilling to reply. There was an almost identical number of references by MPs to other qualities in Priorities 1 to 4 as there were to the base qualities – 60 and 69 citations, respectively. The range of choice and ingenuity is evident in the fact that Priority 1 was scattered among no less than 17 qualities, 6 of the base type, 11 other; with 35 MPs responding, then, this is an average of barely 2 per quality of leadership.

The qualities stressed by MPs as top priority for a Prime Minister were Strong Leadership (4) and Effective Leadership (3), really 7 combined; Maintaining North-South Unity (4), Intellectual Distinction (4); and Ability to Deal With States, National Outlook, and Boldness, Courage and Dynamism (3 each). In terms of simple frequency for Priorities 1 to 4, with more than 7 references, the ranking of MP attitudes was as follows: Effective Leadership (12), Strong Leadership (11), Holding Congress Together (11), Maintaining North-South Unity (9), National Image (8), and Integrity (8). In the case of 2 qualities with a relatively high frequency count, MPs seemed much less concerned than other élite groups – Ability to Solve Economic Problems (only 5 MPs compared to 14 Others) and Ability to Deal With States (5 MPs, 8 Others). However, more than twice as many MPs considered National Image a requisite quality than did Others.

Congress leaders, by contrast, revealed an almost total lack of consensus and a wide range of emphasis on the outstanding quality necessary for India's PM in 1967. The 4 Cabinet Ministers who replied to the question each selected a different quality as Priority 1: Maintaining North-South Unity, Ability to Deal With States, Mass Contact and Support, and Empathy for the Indian Spirit. Working Committee members showed the same pluralism as their governmental colleagues in choosing the most important quality: Strong Leadership (2), and National Image, Holding Congress Together, Harmony With Party Leaders, and Inspiration to People (1 each). In terms of simple frequency, the only quality mentioned by more than 1 Cabinet Minister was Effective Leadership (2). The Working Committee put its greatest stress on Strong Leadership, cited by 4, then Effective Leadership (2), and Holding the Congress Together (2).

The Defeated, Disillusioned and Ex-(DDE) Congressmen shared with Opposition leaders the stress on Ability to Solve Economic Problems, 3 out of 4, and 3 out of 5 respectively, among those who replied. The Opposition placed equal stress on Integrity, and 2 of them each mentioned Intellectual Distinction and Inspiration to the People; 2 of the DDE Congressmen also cited Strong Leadership. Significant in this context is that 6 of the 9 Opposition and DDE Congressmen, who may be grouped together, i.e., *two thirds of the non-Congress élite members stessed the skill of handling economic problems,* while *only* 5 of the 35 MPs and 2 of the 10 Congress leaders, i.e., *7 of the 45 Congressmen stressed this quality.*

There remains the nonpolitical élites. Academics, like Congress leaders, spread their first priority widely: Effective Leadership, National Outlook, Flexibility, Intellectual Distinction, Maintaining North-South Unity, and Pragmatism. In terms of total frequency the Academics revealed greater concentration: Effective Leadership (4), National Outlook (3), and 2 each for Holding Congress Together, Flexibility, Ability to Deal With States, Liberal, Modern Outlook, and Intellectual Distinction.

Among Indian Journalists, too, there is a wide spread. Priority 1 was given to Effective Leadership (2) and Mass Contact (2), and 1 each to Holding Congress Together, Ability to Solve Economic Problems, Boldness, Courage and Dynamism, Acumen, and Restoration of *Swadeshi* Spirit. In terms of over-all frequency, two qualities stand out: Effective (5) and Strong (2) Leadership (7) and the Ability to Solve Economic Problems (6 of 7); great stress is placed on these qualities by the communications élite.

Certain significant points of convergence (shared emphasis) *and divergence* (contrasting emphasis) *emerge from this analysis of group choice* of leadership qualities:

1. *Both segments of the Congress community of respondents placed greatest stress on Effective and Strong Leadership,* measured by frequency of Priority 1 and total frequency count.

2. *Both segments of the Congress élite share with the two nonpolitical élite groups this stress on Effective and Strong Leadership.*

3. *The two segments of the political élite diverge in their emphasis:* Non-Congress respondents emphasize the Ability to Solve Economic Problems, while Congress respondents

stress Effective and Strong Leadership. The ratio of élite reference to the leadership quality of Ability to Solve Economic Problems — by non-Congress and Congress respondents — is 4 to 1. In other words, *the incumbent élite does not appear to place a high value on economic prosperity and growth; the competing élites do.*

4. *One nonpolitical élite group, Indian Journalists, shares with the non-Congress political groups a stress on the Ability to Solve Economic Problems.*

5. *Congress MPs' initiating replies reveal a cluster of qualities; so too those of the non-Congress political élite groups. All other groups reveal a wide spread (pluralism) in their distribution of choice of leadership qualities.*

6. *No one appears to attach any importance to the Foreign Affairs sphere of public policy.*

TABLE 11 : 1*

RANKING OF CONGRESS CANDIDATES FOR THE PRIME MINISTERSHIP

NATIONAL IMAGE

	Mrs. Gandhi		Desai		Chavan		Kamaraj	
Ranked 1	44	*(19)*	18	*(11)*	4	*(3)*	11	*(5)*
Ranked 2	10	*(6)*	18	*(6)*	13	*(9)*	9	*(4)*
Ranked 3	6	*(3)*	15	*(7)*	14	*(8)*	13	*(5)*
Ranked 4	7	*(6)*	15	*(9)*	34	*(13)*	28	*(15)*
TOTAL	67	*(34)*	66	*(33)*	65	*(33)*	61	*(29)*

*Notes: 1. This note applies to Tables 11:1 to 11:15.

2. Figures show frequency distribution in numbers of answers.

3. Figures in brackets refer to the MP component of the figures beside them.

4. There may be discrepancies between total number of respondents and answers in any one rank (lateral summation), for entry of multiple candidates' names in one rank was permitted.

5. The most reliable ranks are 1 and 2. Respondents, that is,those who replied, almost invariably indicated a clear first and second choice for each quality. Many were vague about Ranks 3 and 4. It is recognized by the author that many other variations of ranking were possible. The simple, unweighted scale of 1 to 4, however, serves the analytic purpose of this section of the project to indicate the choice for Prime Minister among the élite respondents and the approximate lead over other candidates.

6. The sample, as in all tables, totalled 80. However, 9 interviewees declined to participate in any part of the ranking. In addition, some failed to rank one or more candidates in any one quality, while others did not rank an entire quality. Thus vertical totals are never more than 71 and are usually less.

TABLE 11 : 2

RANKING OF CONGRESS CANDIDATES FOR THE PRIME MINISTERSHIP

INTERNATIONAL IMAGE

	Mrs. Gandhi		Desai		Chavan		Kamaraj	
Ranked 1	60	(30)	8	(5)	0	(0)	3	(1)
Ranked 2	5	(3)	21	(14)	11	(8)	14	(4)
Ranked 3	1	(1)	13	(8)	12	(8)	8	(4)
Ranked 4	3	(0)	22	(6)	41	(17)	35	(20)
TOTAL	69	(34)	64	(33)	64	(33)	60	(29)

TABLE 11 : 3

RANKING OF CONGRESS CANDIDATES FOR THE PRIME MINISTERSHIP

HOLDING CONGRESS TOGETHER

	Mrs. Gandhi		Desai		Chavan		Kamaraj	
Ranked 1	21	(15)	15	(11)	12	(7)	26	(10)
Ranked 2	13	(4)	12	(7)	12	(9)	5	(5)
Ranked 3	9	(5)	14	(10)	9	(3)	7	(6)
Ranked 4	23	(10)	24	(6)	32	(15)	25	(10)
TOTAL	66	(34)	65	(34)	65	(34)	63	(31)

TABLE 11 : 4

RANKING OF CONGRESS CANDIDATES FOR THE PRIME MINISTERSHIP

MAINTAINING NORTH-SOUTH UNITY

	Mrs. Gandhi		Desai		Chavan		Kamaraj	
Ranked 1	54	(25)	8	(4)	6	(4)	12	(7)
Ranked 2	7	(4)	7	(3)	15	(9)	16	(7)
Ranked 3	6	(3)	21	(13)	17	(7)	6	(2)
Ranked 4	4	(2)	34	(14)	32	(14)	30	(14)
TOTAL	71	(34)	70	(34)	70	(34)	64	(30)

TABLE 11 : 5

RANKING OF CONGRESS CANDIDATES FOR THE PRIME MINISTERSHIP

SATISFACTORY TO MINORITIES

	Mrs. Gandhi		Desai		Chavan		Kamaraj	
Ranked 1	65	(30)	7	(3)	2	(0)	14	(6)
Ranked 2	4	(3)	7	(4)	12	(10)	21	(7)
Ranked 3	0	(0)	15	(8)	16	(10)	8	(6)
Ranked 4	1	(0)	39	(18)	38	(13)	22	(11)
TOTAL	70	(33)	68	(33)	68	(33)	65	(30)

TABLE 11 : 6

RANKING OF CONGRESS CANDIDATES FOR THE PRIME MINISTERSHIP

EFFECTIVE LEADERSHIP

	Mrs. Gandhi		Desai		Chavan		Kamaraj	
Ranked 1	24	(12)	30	(14)	11	(8)	7	(4)
Ranked 2	9	(7)	11	(6)	22	(9)	7	(2)
Ranked 3	11	(7)	12	(7)	13	(8)	7	(3)
Ranked 4	23	(6)	15	(5)	22	(7)	43	(20)
TOTAL	67	(32)	68	(32)	68	(32)	64	(29)

TABLE 11 : 7

RANKING OF CONGRESS CANDIDATES FOR THE PRIME MINISTERSHIP

STRONG LEADER

	Mrs. Gandhi		Desai		Chavan		Kamaraj	
Ranked 1	6	(4)	50	(21)	9	(7)	12	(4)
Ranked 2	10	(7)	9	(6)	19	(13)	12	(3)
Ranked 3	17	(12)	2	(2)	19	(8)	10	(5)
Ranked 4	33	(10)	7	(4)	20	(5)	28	(18)
TOTAL	66	(33)	68	(33)	67	(33)	62	(30)

TABLE 11 : 8

RANKING OF CONGRESS CANDIDATES FOR THE PRIME MINISTERSHIP

FLEXIBLE LEADER

	Mrs. Gandhi		Desai		Chavan		Kamaraj	
Ranked 1	49	(26)	4	(4)	23	(10)	14	(4)
Ranked 2	9	(3)	4	(3)	23	(15)	12	(4)
Ranked 3	6	(3)	6	(3)	12	(4)	20	(13)
Ranked 4	6	(2)	54	(23)	13	(5)	18	(10)
TOTAL	70	(34)	68	(33)	71	(34)	64	(31)

TABLE 11 : 9

RANKING OF CONGRESS CANDIDATES FOR THE PRIME MINISTERSHIP

ABILITY TO DEAL WITH THE OPPOSITION

	Mrs. Gandhi		Desai		Chavan		Kamaraj	
Ranked 1	8	(7)	32	(18)	28	(10)	6	(4)
Ranked 2	16	(7)	13	(4)	23	(14)	4	(0)
Ranked 3	23	(12)	9	(5)	11	(6)	4	(1)
Ranked 4	24	(8)	17	(7)	9	(4)	50	(25)
TOTAL	71	(34)	71	(34)	71	(34)	64	(30)

TABLE 11 : 10

RANKING OF CONGRESS CANDIDATES FOR THE PRIME MINISTERSHIP

ABILITY TO DEAL WITH THE STATES

	Mrs. Gandhi		Desai		Chavan		Kamaraj	
Ranked 1	38	*(18)*	16	*(8)*	21	*(10)*	6	*(1)*
Ranked 2	10	*(4)*	9	*(5)*	17	*(10)*	10	*(4)*
Ranked 3	6	*(4)*	18	*(11)*	14	*(8)*	6	*(3)*
Ranked 4	14	*(7)*	21	*(8)*	13	*(5)*	38	*(23)*
TOTAL	68	*(33)*	64	*(32)*	65	*(33)*	60	*(31)*

TABLE 11 : 11

RANKING OF CONGRESS CANDIDATES FOR THE PRIME MINISTERSHIP

HARMONY WITH PARTY (CONGRESS) LEADERS

	Mrs. Gandhi		Desai		Chavan		Kamaraj	
Ranked 1	22	*(15)*	3	*(3)*	12	*(6)*	26	*(9)*
Ranked 2	18	*(8)*	5	*(2)*	16	*(9)*	8	*(6)*
Ranked 3	6	*(1)*	18	*(11)*	12	*(7)*	7	*(4)*
Ranked 4	17	*(8)*	36	*(16)*	23	*(10)*	21	*(11)*
TOTAL	63	*(32)*	62	*(32)*	63	*(32)*	62	*(30)*

TABLE 11 : 12

RANKING OF CONGRESS CANDIDATES FOR THE PRIME MINISTERSHIP

IMPLEMENTATION OF A SOCIALIST PROGRAM

	Mrs. Gandhi		Desai		Chavan		Kamaraj	
Ranked 1	20	*(12)*	7	*(4)*	9	*(7)*	30	*(14)*
Ranked 2	16	*(11)*	4	*(4)*	13	*(6)*	11	*(6)*
Ranked 3	10	*(3)*	4	*(2)*	17	*(11)*	6	*(6)*
Ranked 4	19	*(8)*	49	*(23)*	26	*(10)*	15	*(5)*
TOTAL	65	*(34)*	64	*(33)*	65	*(34)*	62	*(31)*

TABLE 11 : 13

RANKING OF CONGRESS CANDIDATES FOR THE PRIME MINISTERSHIP

PROVIDING A BETTER CLIMATE FOR BUSINESS

	Mrs. Gandhi		Desai		Chavan		Kamaraj	
Ranked 1	23	(7)	41	(19)	6	(3)	3	(1)
Ranked 2	9	(4)	7	(4)	25	(16)	4	(2)
Ranked 3	17	(13)	4	(2)	13	(3)	5	(3)
Ranked 4	13	(6)	10	(5)	15	(7)	43	(20)
TOTAL	62	(30)	62	(30)	59	(29)	55	(26)

TABLE 11 : 14

RANKING OF CONGRESS CANDIDATES FOR THE PRIME MINISTERSHIP

ABILITY TO SOLVE ECONOMIC PROBLEMS

	Mrs. Gandhi		Desai		Chavan		Kamaraj	
Ranked 1	12	(8)	37	(16)	13	(8)	14	(7)
Ranked 2	8	(7)	7	(5)	14	(10)	10	(2)
Ranked 3	14	(8)	8	(6)	7	(2)	5	(3)
Ranked 4	33	(10)	15	(5)	32	(13)	34	(18)
TOTAL	67	(33)	67	(32)	66	(33)	63	(30)

TABLE 11 : 15

RANKING OF CONGRESS CANDIDATES FOR THE PRIME MINISTERSHIP

FOREIGN POLICY

	Mrs. Gandhi		Desai		Chavan		Kamaraj	
Ranked 1	39	(25)	16	(5)	8	(4)	5	(0)
Ranked 2	7	(4)	18	(14)	17	(10)	6	(4)
Ranked 3	4	(0)	9	(6)	13	(8)	8	(5)
Ranked 4	20	(5)	25	(8)	31	(12)	45	(22)
TOTAL	70	(34)	68	(33)	69	(34)	64	(31)

TABLE 11 : 16

RANKING OF CONGRESS CANDIDATES FOR THE PRIME MINISTERSHIP

MRS. GANDHI

CRITERIA	in which the Candidate Ranked Best Qualified		in which the Candidate Ranked Worst Qualified	
	Number of Respondents	Percentage of Total	Number of Respondents	Percentage of Total
National Image	44	55.0	7	8.7
International Image	60	75.0	3	3.7
Holding Congress Together	21	26.2	23	28.8
Maintaining North-South Unity	54	67.5	4	5.0
Satisfactory to Minorities	65	81.3	1	1.2
Effective Leadership	24	30.0	23	28.7
Strong Leader	6	7.5	33	41.2
Flexible Leader	49	61.2	6	7.5
Ability to Deal With Opposition	8	10.0	24	30.0
Ability to Deal With States	38	47.5	14	17.5
Harmony with Party Leaders	22	27.5	17	21.2
Implementation of Socialist Program	20	25.0	19	23.7
Providing a Better Business Climate	23	28.7	13	16.2
Ability to Solve Economic Problems	12	15.0	33	41.2
Foreign Policy	39	48.7	20	25.0

TABLE 11 : 17

RANKING OF CONGRESS CANDIDATES FOR THE PRIME MINISTERSHIP

DESAI

CRITERIA	in which the Candidate Ranked Best Qualified		in which the Candidate Ranked Worst Qualified	
	Number of Respondents	Percentage of Total	Number of Respondents	Percentage of Total
National Image	18	22.5	15	18.8
International Image	8	10.0	22	27.5
Holding Congress Together	15	18.8	24	30.0
Maintaining North-South Unity	8	10.0	34	42.5
Satisfactory to Minorities	7	8.7	39	48.7
Effective Leadership	30	37.5	15	18.8
Strong Leader	50	62.5	7	8.7
Flexible Leader	4	5.0	54	67.5
Ability to Deal With Opposition	32	40.0	17	21.2
Ability to Deal With States	16	20.0	21	26.2
Harmony with Party Leaders	3	3.7	36	45.0
Implementation of Socialist Program	7	8.7	49	61.2
Providing a Better Business Climate	41	51.2	10	12.5
Ability to Solve Economic Problems	37	46.2	15	18.8
Foreign Policy	16	20.0	25	31.3

TABLE 11 : 18

RANKING OF CONGRESS CANDIDATES FOR THE PRIME MINISTERSHIP

CHAVAN

CRITERIA	in which the Candidate Ranked Best Qualified		in which the Candidate Ranked Worst Qualified	
	Number of Respondents	Percentage of Total	Number of Respondents	Percentage of Total
National Image	4	5.0	34	42.5
International Image	0	0.0	41	51.2
Holding Congress Together	12	15.0	32	40.0
Maintaining North-South Unity	6	7.5	32	40.0
Satisfactory to Minorities	2	2.5	38	47.5
Effective Leadership	11	13.7	22	27.5
Strong Leader	9	11.2	20	25.0
Flexible Leader	23	28.7	13	16.2
Ability to Deal With Opposition	28	35.0	9	11.2
Ability to Deal With States	21	26.2	13	16.2
Harmony with Party Leaders	12	15.0	23	28.7
Implementation of Socialist Program	9	11.2	26	32.5
Providing a Better Business Climate	6	7.5	15	18.8
Ability to Solve Economic Problems	13	16.2	32	40.0
Foreign Policy	8	10.0	31	38.7

TABLE 11 : 19

RANKING OF CONGRESS CANDIDATES FOR THE PRIME MINISTERSHIP

KAMARAJ

CRITERIA	in which the Candidate Ranked Best Qualified		in which the Candidate Ranked Worst Qualified	
	Number of Respondents	Percentage of Total	Number of Respondents	Percentage of Total
National Image	11	13.7	28	35.0
International Image	3	3.7	35	43.8
Holding Congress Together	26	32.5	25	31.3
Maintaining North-South Unity	12	15.0	30	37.5
Satisfactory to Minorities	14	17.5	22	27.5
Effective Leadership	7	8.7	43	53.7
Strong Leader	12	15.0	28	35.0
Flexible Leader	14	17.5	18	22.5
Ability to Deal With Opposition	6	7.5	50	62.5
Ability to Deal With States	6	7.5	38	47.5
Harmony with Party Leaders	26	32.5	21	26.2
Implementation of Socialist Program	30	37.5	15	18.8
Providing a Better Business Climate	3	3.7	43	53.7
Ability to Solve Economic Problems	14	17.5	34	42.5
Foreign Policy	5	6.3	45	56.3

According to the scale data in Tables 11:1 — 11:15, Mrs. Gandhi ranks first in 7 qualities (Qs) for the Prime Ministership, almost half of the total (15). Morarji Desai received the largest number of Rank 1 rating in 5 Qs, Kamaraj in 3, and Chavan in 0. At the other extreme, Kamaraj has the highest Rank 4 frequency in 6 Qs, 40 per cent of the total, Desai in 5, Chavan in 3, and Mrs. Gandhi in 1 quality. Thus, *the distribution of Rank 1 and Rank 4* (best and least qualified) *based on a frequency count, reveals a clear preference for Mrs. Gandhi among the Indian élite respondents. Desai is undoubtedly the second over-all choice, Kamaraj and Chavan are bunched, with the former having a conspicuous advantage in Rank 1 frequency and the latter in Rank 4.*

A corrective, indeed, the most accurate over-all élite assessment, emerges from *pairs ranking* within each quality. If one combines the frequency count in Ranks 1 and 4, the rating of the best and least qualified Congress candidates for the Prime Ministership would be as follows:

ELITE EVALUATION OF THE MAJOR CANDIDATES ON THEIR ABILITIES
TO MEET THE REQUIREMENTS OF PRIME MINISTER

Quality	Best Qualified	Ranks 1—4	Least Qualified	Ranks 1—4
National Image	Mrs. Gandhi	44—7	Chavan	4—34
International Image	Mrs. Gandhi	60—3	Chavan	0—41
Holding Congress Together	Kamaraj	26—25	Chavan	12—32
Maintaining North-South Unity	Mrs. Gandhi	54—4	Chavan	6—32
			Desai	8—34
Satisfactory to Minorities	Mrs. Gandhi	65—1	Chavan	2—38
Effective Leadership	Desai	30—15	Kamaraj	7—43
Strong Leader	Desai	50—7	Mrs. Gandhi	6—33
Flexible Leader	Mrs. Gandhi	49—6	Desai	4—54
Ability to Deal with Opposition	Desai	32—17	Kamaraj	6—50
	Chavan	28—9		

Quality	Best Qualified	Ranks 1 - 4	Least Qualified	Ranks 1 - 4
Ability to Deal with States	Mrs. Gandhi	38—14	Kamaraj	6—38
Harmony with Party Leaders	Kamaraj	26—21	Desai	3—36
Implementation of Socialist Program	Kamaraj	30—15	Desai	7—49
Providing a Better Climate for Business	Desai	41—10	Kamaraj	3—43
Ability to Solve Economic Problems	Desai	37—15	Mrs. Gandhi	12—33
			Chavan	13—32
			Kamaraj	14—34
Pursuing Successful Foreign Policy	Mrs. Gandhi	39—20	Kamaraj	5—45

In the revised distribution of "best qualified," Mrs. Gandhi, Kamaraj, and Chavan are unchanged, 7, 3, and 0 Qs respectively, while Desai's primacy declines from 5 to 4 Qs. In the remaining 1 Q, there is a virtual tie: Desai and Chavan, in the Ability to Deal with the Opposition in Parliament. There is also a corrective in the distribution of "least qualified": Desai sheds this rating in 2 Qs, and Kamaraj in 1, while Chavan adds 1 Q; Chavan and Desai are very close in the category Maintaining North-South Unity, while Mrs. Gandhi, Chavan, and Kamaraj are regarded as almost identical in the Ability to Solve Economic Problems. In summary, then,

CORRECTED DATA ON BEST QUALIFIED AND LEAST QUALIFIED

Best Qualified		Least Qualified	
Mrs. Gandhi	7	Kamaraj	5 (+1 tie)
Desai	4 (+1 tie)	Chavan	4 (+2 ties)
Kamaraj	3	Desai	3 (+1 tie)
Chavan	0 (+1 tie)	Mrs. Gandhi	1 (+1 tie)

The evidence is unmistakable: *Mrs. Gandhi was the overwhelming choice of the Indian élite sample as the best qualified Congress leader for the position of Prime Minister; Desai was the second choice, with Kamaraj close behind, and Chavan at the other extreme.* This conclusion, however, is based purely on the *number of categories* in which the candidates were rated best-and least-qualified. It is necessary to probe further into the strengths and weaknesses of each Congress leader as evaluated by the élite respondents.

MRS. GANDHI

Judged by the pairs ranking, Mrs. Gandhi has the best image within India as a whole and in the world at large. She would contribute most to the maintenance of North-South unity and is the most trusted by India's minorities. She is regarded as the most flexible Congress leader and the ablest in dealing with the states. She is also rated the most highly skilled in the realm of foreign policy.

Perhaps the best indication of her pre-eminence in the over-all élite rating of Congress leaders is the margin she enjoys in 6 of these 7 categories.

National Image (Table 11:1)

She was ranked first by 44 persons, 55 per cent of the total — and two thirds of the actual — number of respondents. Stated in terms of ratio, the number of interviewees who ranked her first compared to Morarji Desai's Rank 1 was 2.5 to 1; it was 4 to 1 compared to Kamaraj and 11 to 1 compared to Chavan. Similarly, at the other end of the scale, she is regarded as the person with the least impressive all-India image by less than half as many who so ranked Morarji, one fourth compared to Kamaraj and one fifth relative to Chavan. There was *no doubt whatever in this category.*

International Image (Table 11:2)

There is even less doubt on this Q. No fewer than 60 persons ranked her first — 75 per cent of the total respondents and 85 per cent of those who actually replied. The ratio between her and Morarji Desai is 7.5 to 1 and between her and Kamaraj 20 to 1. Not a single person ranked Chavan first. *The consensus is overwhelming.*

Maintaining North-South Unity (Table 11:4)

Mrs. Gandhi's *margin of superiority in this Q is not quite so pronounced but very great nonetheless* — 54 in Rank 1, i.e., two thirds of the total sample, more than 75 per cent of those who replied. The spread between her Rank 1 frequency and the other Congress leaders is striking: 4.5 to 1 compared to Kamaraj, almost 7 to 1 relative to Desai, and 9 to 1 in the case of Chavan. Only 4 of 71 respondents regarded her as least qualified in this respect; all other candidates ranged from 7.5 to 8.5 times as many in the least qualified rank.

Satisfactory to Minorities (Table 11:5)

In this sphere Mrs. Gandhi's margin was greatest — 65 in Rank 1, i.e., 81 per cent of the total and more than 90 per cent of those who replied. Her closest rival was Kamaraj, with 14 in Rank 1; for Desai it was 7, and for Chavan 2. The margin in favor of Mrs. Gandhi was, respectively, 4.7 to 1, 9.3 to 1, and 32.5 to 1. The ratios in Rank 4 are even greater, for only 1 respondent regarded Mrs. Gandhi as least qualified.

Flexible Leader (Table 11:8)

Mrs. Gandhi has a clear majority in this leadership quality, but the distribution is less sharp than in the 3 preceding Qs; *the pattern is,* rather, *similar to that on National Image.* Mrs. Gandhi was given the Rank 1 rating by 49 respondents, i.e., 61 per cent of the total, and 70 per cent of the actual number of persons who replied. Her closest rival was Chavan with 23, and then, Kamaraj and Desai with 14 and 4 each. Thus the ratio of top rating in this sphere between her and the other Congress leaders was slightly more than 2 to 1, 3.7 to 1, and 12 to 1, respectively. Similar ratios obtain at the lower end of the scale. In short, *Mrs. Gandhi enjoyed a comfortable but not overwhelming majority.*

Ability to Deal With the States (Table 11:10)

Mrs. Gandhi's margin of superiority is *lowest in this sphere* – 38 in Rank 1, i.e., 47.5 per cent of the total and 55 per cent of the actual replies. Chavan showed considerable strength here (21) and Desai as well (16). Thus the ratios between Mrs. Gandhi's Rank 1 frequency and that of the other Congress leaders is 1.8 to 1 relative to Chavan, 2.4 to 1 relative to Desai, and 6 to 1 relative to Kamaraj. No less significant than this flatter distribution for Rank 1 is the fact that more persons rated Mrs. Gandhi least qualified than they did Chavan – 14 to 13; and Desai was not far behind, 21. In short, *no single Congress leader was regarded as pre-eminent in this Q.*

Foreign Policy (Table 11:15)

Mrs. Gandhi's Rank 1 frequency is just short of a majority of the total respondents (39 of 80, i.e., 48.7 per cent); but it is 55 per cent of the actual number of persons who replied. More pointed are the ratios in Rank 1 frequency: 2.5 to 1 compared to Desai, almost 5 to 1 relative to Chavan, and almost 8 to 1 relative to Kamaraj. Her margin of superiority in this sphere is very similar to that in Ability to Deal with the States – *not overwhelming but undoubted.* And yet 20 persons, almost 30 per cent of those who replied, rated Mrs. Gandhi least qualified in this sphere.

Summary

Mrs. Gandhi showed *great strength (a decisive majority)* in the following Qs: Satisfactory to Minorities, International Image, and Maintaining North-South Unity. The élite accorded her a *clear majority* in regard to Flexibility and National Image, and a *plurality (limited strength)* in the Ability to Deal With the States, as well as Foreign Policy.

Apart from these 7 categories of strength, there are two areas in which Mrs. Gandhi was rated weak – Strong Leadership and the Ability to Solve Economic Problems.

Strong Leader (Table 11:7)

The *élite assessment of Mrs. Gandhi in this* Q — which most of the élite groups considered of great importance — was one of *overwhelming nonconfidence.* Only 6 persons accorded her Rank 1, i.e., 7.5 per cent of the total, and 9 per cent of the actual respondents. The ratio to Morarji's Rank 1 frequency is 1 to 8.3. No less pointed is the fact that *more respondents thought her least qualified in this respect than any of the 3 other Congress leaders;* 33 persons, or 50 per cent of those who replied, so regarded her.

Ability to Solve Economic Problems (Table 11:14)

In this important sphere, too, Mrs. Gandhi's Rank 1 frequency is the lowest among the 4 leaders — but the distribution is relatively even for 3 persons — 12 (Mrs. Gandhi), 13 (Chavan) and 14 (Kamaraj). And though her Rank 4 frequency is a shade higher than for Chavan, Kamaraj. is even higher. *None of these 3 leaders was considered well qualified in the economic policy sphere.* Indeed, only Desai was rated highly in this critical area of leadership.

DESAI

The man who contested the Prime Ministership unsuccessfully in 1964, 1966, and 1967, was ranked "best qualified" in four areas — Effective Leadership, Strong Leadership, Providing a Better Climate for Business, and Ability to Solve Economic Problems. In the first, he was accorded a modest plurality; in the second, a decisive majority; in the third, a marginal majority; and in the fourth, a substantial plurality.

Effective Leadership (Table 11:6)

Morarji Desai was ranked first by 30 persons, i.e., 37.5 per cent of the total and 45 per cent of the actual respondents. His closest rival, Mrs. Gandhi, had a Rank 1 frequency of 24, i.e., a ratio of 1.25 to 1; but he was markedly ahead of the other leaders, 3 to 1 relative to Chavan and 4.3 to 1 relative to Kamaraj. More pointed was the relative ratio of Ranks 1 and 4 of Morarji and his competitors: 2 to 1 in favor of best qualified for him, 1 to 1 for Mrs. Gandhi. In short, *Desai was the clear but not decisive choice of the élite for most effective leadership.*

Strong Leader (Table 11:7)

Desai's towering position in this Q is evident in the data. He received a Rank 1 frequency of 50, i.e., 62.5 per cent of the total, 75 per cent of the actual respondents; all other candidates are bunched together; the ratio of his majority is 4.2 to 1 relative to Kamaraj, 5.5 to 1 relative to Chavan, and 8.3 to 1 relative to Mrs. Gandhi. Only 7 ranked Desai "least qualified," while the lowest comparable frequency was 20 — for Chavan. *The élite consensus that Morarji was the strongest leader of the 4 is clearly demonstrated.*

Providing a Better Climate for Business (Table 11:13)

Desai's Rank 1 frequency in this Q is half way between that in Effective and Strong Leadership — a marginal majority of the total respondents (41 of 80) and 66 per cent of the actual number who replied. The closest of the other 3 leaders in Rank 1 frequency is Mrs. Gandhi, with 23, but Desai outnumbers all 3 combined (41 to 32). This rating is not unexpected in the light of Desai's long-standing identification with conservatism; one might have expected a greater consensus.

Ability to Solve Economic Problems (Table 11:14)

In one sense, Desai's margin of superiority is lower here than in the preceding Q — only 37 in Rank 1, i.e., 46.2 per cent of the total, and 55 per cent of the actual respondents. In another sense, however, the superiority is more pronounced; all other leaders are bunched together, and Desai has approximately a 3 to 1 ratio in Rank 1 frequency, for all of them. This reflects a widely articulated view among the respondents that the other 3 persons were not capable of dealing effectively with economic problems. Desai may have lacked an absolute majority, but he was *the overwhelming relative choice* of the élite *in this sphere.*

The élite assessment of *Morarji's weakness* extends over three areas of leadership: flexibility, relations with other Congress leaders, and the implementation of a socialist program.

Flexible Leadership (Table 11:8)

As might be expected, the frequency of Ranks 1 and 4 for Desai (and for Mrs. Gandhi) in this category and in the Q, Strong Leadership, are reversed. Whereas in the latter, it was 50-7 for Desai, in the Q, Flexibility, it was 4-54. Thus, only 5 per cent of the total or 6 per cent of the actual respondents gave him Rank 1, while 80 per cent of the actual replies accorded him "least qualified" ranking. Relative to Mrs. Gandhi, his Rank 1 frequency was 1 to 12, to Chavan, 1 to 6 and to Kamaraj, 1 to 3. *The deep-rooted image of Desai as inflexible is starkly reflected in this élite rating.*

Harmony with Party (Congress) Leaders (Table 11:11)

Desai's low rating here is a corollary of the above data. Many of his colleagues, and rank-and-file Congressmen as well, view him as unbending and committed to what he regards as principle, even if harmony within the·leadership is adversely affected. Thus only 3 gave him Rank 1, a mere 3.7 per cent of the total or 5 per cent of the actual respondents. Compared with his competitors the ratio in Rank 1 was 1 to 4 relative to Chavan, 1 to 7 relative to Mrs. Gandhi, and 1 to 9 relative to Kamaraj. Moreover, 60 per cent of the actual replies termed him "least qualified" in this respect. *Images within the Indian élites are not easily changed.*

Implementation of a Socialist Program (Table 11:12)

The élite assessment of Desai in this area of policy is not surprising, for he has long been identified as a leader of the right.

Thus only 7 gave him Rank 1, about 9 per cent of the total, and 11 per cent of the actual respondents. He shared this low frequency with Chavan, but the ratio to Mrs. Gandhi was 1 to 3 and to Kamaraj, 1 to 4.3. More pointed is the fact that 49 persons, three quarters of the actual replies, termed him least likely to implement a socialist program. *Once more, deep-rooted images were reflected in the élite assessment.*

Summary

Desai was rated by the élite sample as the strongest and most effective of the 4 possible Congress candidates for Prime Minister. He was also regarded as the most trusted by the business community and the most skilled in dealing with economic problems. At the same time, he was judged to be the least flexible, the least qualified to maintain harmony with Congress leaders, and the least likely to implement a socialist program.

KAMARAJ

The Congress President was given the highest relative rating in three categories, but in none of these was it a majority of the total — or even — actual respondents.

Holding Congress Together (Table 11:3)

In this Q, Kamaraj exceeded his nearest rival, Mrs. Gandhi, by only 5 in Rank 1 (26 to 21); there is indeed a rather flat distribution pattern, with 15 for Desai and 12 for Chavan. Also indicative of the blurred élite assessment is the fact that almost as many persons (25) rated Kamaraj "least qualified," a shade more than the Rank 4 frequency for Mrs. Gandhi or Desai. The data in this table reflected *a widely shared (and widely expressed) view that no one Congress leader could keep the party together; only cooperation among the four could achieve this.*

Harmony With Party (Congress) Leaders (Table 11:11)

A similar situation obtains in this closely related Q: Kamaraj
secured 26 in Rank 1, only one third of the total, and 42 per cent of
the actual number of respondents; and his closest rival, Mrs. Gandhi,
received 22. The curve is much sharper, however, for Desai was rated
best qualified by only 3 persons. That the élite doubted Kamaraj's
ability in this sphere is also evident in the fact that almost as many,
21 persons, rated him least qualified – more than so rated Mrs.
Gandhi. *Here, too, cooperation among the leaders, especially
between Kamaraj and Mrs. Gandhi, was considered essential.*

Implementation of Socialist Program (Table 11:12)

Kamaraj has a *more conspicuous plurality* in this area, but by no
means decisive. His Rank 1 frequency is 30, i.e., 37.5 per cent of the
total, and a shade below 50 per cent of the actual number of
respondents. The spread between his Rank 1 frequency and all his
rivals is greater than in the other 2 Qs in which he ranked best
qualified: 1.5 to 1 relative to Mrs. Gandhi, 3.3 to 1 relative to
Chavan, and 4.3 to 1 relative to Desai. Moreover, twice as many
persons rated him best qualified as did least qualified. In short,
*among the four Congress leaders, Kamaraj was regarded as the most
likely to implement the long-held Congress commitment to socialism
– if he were in power – but only a minority of respondents thought
that even he would do so.*
     The incumbent Congress President was also rated least qualified
in 5 Qs, and *in 4 of them the adverse assessment was overwhelming –
much more so than in the 3 above-noted areas where he was
accorded the top rank.*

Effective Leadership (Table 11:6)

Only 7 ranked Kamaraj first in this vital Q, 8.7 per cent of the
total and only 11 per cent of the persons who replied. Compared to
the Rank 1 rating for Desai, it was 1 to 4.3, and relative to Mrs.

Gandhi's rating, it was 1 to 3.5. More pointed is the staggering figure of 43 who rated him least qualified, two thirds of the actual respondents, and double the frequency for Mrs. Gandhi and Chavan. Clearly Kamaraj was regarded as the least effective of the four Congress leaders.

Ability to Deal With Opposition (in Parliament) (Table 11:9)

Kamaraj's rating in this Q is even more adverse. Only 6 gave him Rank 1, 7.5 per cent of the total, and 10 per cent of the actual respondents. It is true that Mrs. Gandhi did not fare well in this respect (8), but the gap is large, relative to the Rank 1 frequency for Desai and Chavan — 1 to 5.3 and 1 to 4.6. Moreover, no fewer than 50 persons, i.e., 80 per cent of those who replied, regarded him as least qualified; and while the ratio between Ranks 1 and 4 is 1 to 3 for Mrs. Gandhi, it is 1 to 8.3 for Kamaraj, almost three times as much. In short, while *the over-all élite view* was that neither Kamaraj nor Mrs. Gandhi were capable of dealing with the opposition in Parliament, it *was emphatic in rating Kamaraj as much worse qualified* in this respect — largely because of his limited command of English, the working language in Parliament.

Ability to Deal With the States (Table 11:10)

In this area, too, Kamaraj emerges as the clear élite choice for least qualified Congress leader. Only 6 accorded him Rank 1, 10 per cent of those who replied. Unlike the pattern in the preceding table, he does not share this lack of confidence with another leader; as noted earlier, the distribution is flatter for the Rank 1 frequency among the other 3 candidates. Moreover, the ratio of Rank 1 to Rank 4 for Kamaraj is less glaring — but high, nonetheless, 1 to 6.3; and almost two thirds of the actual replies (38 out of 60) rated him least qualified. In short, *while no candidate was given an overwhelming vote of confidence, Kamaraj received an unmistakable vote of nonconfidence.*

Providing a Better Climate for Business (Table 11:13)

Kamaraj's rating in this Q is even more emphatic than in the preceding one. Only 3 persons, the same number as in the area of International Image, ranked him first, i.e., 3.7 per cent of the total, or 5.5 per cent of the actual respondents. Only Chavan is close in negative ranking in this Q (6 in Rank 1), but the ratios of Kamaraj to the others are very pronounced — 1 to 7.7 relative to Mrs. Gandhi and 1 to 13.7 relative to Desai. This is the natural obverse to Kamaraj's high rating in terms of the implementation of a socialist program. The Congress President was regarded as a man of the left and was mistrusted by the business community.

Foreign Policy (Table 11:15)

Here, too, Kamaraj was regarded as the least competent among the four Congress leaders. Only 5 persons ranked him first, i.e., 6.3 per cent of the total, and less than 8 per cent of the actual respondents. Once more Chavan approaches him in paucity of Rank 1 frequency. But the most striking fact is that 45 of the 64 actual respondents, i.e., 70 per cent, ranked Kamaraj least qualified in the foreign policy sphere. In short, there is *a high élite consensus that Kamaraj lacks the skill to deal with India's external relations,* perhaps because of his lack of fluency in English or indeed any language other than Tamil.

Summary

In *summary,* then, Kamaraj was accorded a *plurality Rank 1* in the related organizational Qs, Holding Congress Together and Harmony with Party Leaders; the designation "best qualified" was *more generous* regarding the Implementation of a Socialist Program. He was rated *very poorly* in Effective Leadership, Ability to Deal with the Opposition in Parliament, Ability to Deal with the States, Providing a Better Climate for Business, and as far as Foreign Policy is concerned.

CHAVAN

The Home Minister was rated the best qualified in no sphere — and the least qualified in 4 Qs, some of them of considerable importance. Thus his over-all standing in the élite assessment is last among the four Congress leaders.

National Image (Table 11:1)

Chavan's weakness in this sphere is clearly evident in the data. Only 4 persons ranked him first, a mere 5 per cent of the total, or 6 per cent of the actual respondents. The ratio of his Rank 1 frequency to that of his colleagues is 1 to 3 relative to Kamaraj, 1 to 4.5 relative to Desai, and 1 to 11 relative to Mrs. Gandhi. Not only is his standing last; many respondents referred to him as a "Maharashtrian parochialist," an image which has clung to him during the five years he had been a senior all-India Cabinet Minister, first Defence and then Home. Indeed, *this absence of a National Image has been a major barrier to Chavan's attainment of the Prime Ministership thus far —* in the view of many.

International Image (Table 11:2)

Chavan's rating in this Q is the lowest of all assessments of the four Congress leaders in the 15 categories of leadership. It is also *the only case in which not a single respondent accorded a candidate Rank 1.* Moreover, 41 persons, i.e., two thirds of those who actually replied, ranked Chavan last in International Image. Kamaraj's rating in this sphere was almost as weak, but *Chavan emerges as the least known and least respected Congress leader on the world stage.*

Holding Congress Together (Table 11:3)

Although the least qualified in this sphere, too, Chavan's rating is much less extreme than in the two preceding Qs. His Rank 1 frequency is 12, 15 per cent of the total, and almost 20 per cent of the actual replies. Moreover, it is only a shade less than Desai's frequency (15) in this rank and not very much less than the others (Mrs Gandhi, 21, and Kamaraj, 26). So too in the Rank 4 rating: Half of the actual respondents considered Chavan least qualified in this respect, but the three other candidates received a comparable frequency between 35 and 40 per cent. In short, *Chavan is regarded as the weakest of the four in terms of the goal of Congress unity, but all four are individually weak in this quality.*

Satisfactory to Minorities (Table 11:5)

Once more Chavan's rating is very low. Only 2 persons accord him Rank 1, a mere 3 per cent of the actual number of respondents. Desai's Rank 1 frequency, too, is low (7), but the ratio with others is glaring: 1 to 7 relative to Kamaraj and 1 to 32.5 relative to Mrs. Gandhi. At the lower end of the scale, 38 persons, i.e., 55 per cent of the actual respondents, regard Chavan as least satisfactory to the minorities, but an even larger number (39) so regard Desai. Thus Chavan is viewed as the *least-trusted by India's minorities, a spill-over from his image as a "Maharashtrian parochialist,"* but he shares this élite assessment to a considerable extent with Desai.

Summary

In *summary,* Chavan's International Image is *virtually nil,* according to the élite; his National Image is undermined by his strong ties to Maharashtra; and in 2 other spheres, Holding Congress Together and Satisfactory to Minorities, he is the *weakest but not alone;* all four are relatively unqualified in the former, and Desai shares his status in the latter. Chavan's over-all standing is improved by a *virtual tie* with Desai in the Ability to Deal with the Opposition in Parliament.

ANALYSIS OF SPREAD WITHIN QUALITIES*

National Image. Mrs. Gandhi clearly ranks first, Desai second, Kamaraj third and Chavan fourth. There is an equal spread between Desai and Kamaraj, and between Kamaraj and Chavan. However, the spread between first and second rated leaders is enormous (44 to 18 in Rank 1 frequency). Mrs. Gandhi has one third more frequency in Rank 1 than all others combined.

Whereas Mrs. Gandhi's over-all Rank 1 frequency was almost two thirds of the total actual respondents, the MP component was only 19 out of 34, i.e., 55 per cent. Conversely, the MP component in Desai's over-all Rank 1 frequency was higher (11 out of 34, or 33 per cent) than his proportion of the total actual respondents (18 out of 66, or 27 per cent). In short, the *weightage of MP rating was more in favor of Desai than of Mrs. Gandhi in this Q.*

International Image. Mrs. Gandhi's pre-eminence is much more pronounced. Desai is once more a clear second, with Kamaraj and Chavan sharing the image, least qualified. The best qualified has more than five times the frequency in Rank 1 of all other candidates combined. Her margin of superiority is overwhelming.

Holding Congress Together. The four leaders are bunched together, with an almost equal spread among them in Rank 1 frequency — Kamaraj 26, Mrs. Gandhi 21, Desai 15, and Chavan 12. This reflects the consensus among the Congress rank-and-file and Congress leaders that only cooperation among the four could maintain party unity.

The MP component in Kamaraj's over-all Rank 1 frequency is disproportionately low (32 per cent of the total actual MP respondents compared to 39 per cent of total actual respondents of

---

* The MP component of the over-all figure for each candidate within Rank 1 of each Q is not analyzed in detail. Only where noteworthy deviating tendencies are observed are they included in this brief analysis of the spread within Qs.

all groups indicating him as their first choice). For Mrs. Gandhi, the MP component is proportionately high (44 and 33.3 per cent respectively); and for Desai, it is also higher than for Kamaraj (30 and 23 per cent respectively). Thus, Congress MP's had *greater faith than Others in Mrs. Gandhi's and Desai's ability to hold Congress together than they did in Kamaraj.*

Maintaining North-South Unity. As with Q 2, Mrs. Gandhi's pre-eminence is conspicuous, but the other three leaders are more closely bunched — indicating an élite consensus that only Mrs. Gandhi, of the Congress leaders, had the ability to maintain North-South unity. The spread between her and second-placed Kamaraj is 42, whereas the spread between second and fourth is 6.

Satisfactory to Minorities. Mrs. Gandhi's pre-eminence is pronounced as with Qs 2 and 4. The spread between her and second-placed Kamaraj is enormous, 51 in Rank 1, whereas the spread among the three other leaders averages 6. Her Rank 1 frequency is three times as high as that of the others combined. Only Mrs. Gandhi, according to the élite consensus, enjoyed the trust of India's minorities.

Effective Leadership. Desai was a clear, though not overwhelming choice as best qualified. Mrs. Gandhi was a close second, Chavan third, and Kamaraj fourth. The spread between Desai and Mrs. Gandhi was similar to that between Chavan and Kamaraj, but the first two are clearly set off from the others; second-placed Mrs. Gandhi has more than double the Rank 1 frequency of third-placed Chavan.

Strong Leader. Desai is pre-eminent in this Q, almost as strikingly as Mrs. Gandhi in Q 4 — Maintaining North-South Unity. The other three leaders are bunched together, with a small equal spread: Kamaraj 12, Chavan 9, and Mrs. Gandhi 6. By contrast, the spread between Desai and second place Kamaraj in Rank 1 is 38; Desai was accorded almost double the Rank 1 frequency of the other three leaders combined. The consensus of the élite sample is clear: Desai is the *strongest* of the Congress leaders.

The MP component in Desai's over-all Rank 1 frequency is proportionately low (64 per cent of the total actual MP respondents compared to 73 per cent of the total actual respondents of all groups). Stated in different terms, *Congress MPs were less impressed with Desai's qualifications as a strong leader than were Others.*

Flexible Leader. Mrs. Gandhi is a very clear first choice, but not overwhelmingly so; Chavan is also respected for flexibility. The gap between second and third place is almost identical to that between third and fourth place, 9 and 10 respectively, while the spread between Mrs. Gandhi and Chavan is 26. Nonetheless, Chavan was accorded Rank 1 by almost 30 per cent of the respondents. The distribution is uneven, with two of the four leaders rated highly.

Ability to Deal With the Opposition. The distribution in this Q is very different, with two distinct concentrations. Desai and Chavan share the designation, "best qualified," with 32 and 28 Rank 1 frequency, respectively. It is the former's considerably higher Rank 4 frequency (17 to 9) which suggests *a virtual tie.* Mrs. Gandhi and Kamaraj are concentrated at the other extreme, with 8 and 6 Rank 1 respondents, respectively. Yet Mrs. Gandhi must be rated third because of the much higher "least qualified" designation accorded to Kamaraj (50 to 24). This is one of three qualities with a very close distribution at the top.

Although Desai and Chavan have only a slight difference in over-all Rank 1 frequency, the relative weight of MP rating is markedly different. *For Desai the proportionate influence of the MP component is high* (54 per cent of the total actual MP respondents and 45 per cent of the total actual respondents of all groups). *For Chavan the MP component is relatively low* (30 and 40 per cent respectively).

Ability to Deal with the States. The distribution here is very similar to Q 6 — Effective Leadership, though the spread in Rank 1 is greater between first and second place (38 to 21) and between third and fourth place (16 to 6). In this Q, Mrs. Gandhi is a very clear first choice, with Chavan and Desai close together, and Kamaraj last.

Chavan's claim to second place is enhanced by the Rank 4 frequency — less for him (13) than for Mrs. Gandhi (14) and much less than for Desai (21). The two extremes in the distribution are clear, the middle is bunched.

Harmony With Party Leaders. Once more the distribution is different, with 2 persons bunched at the top and an almost equal spread between second and third and between third and fourth place. Kamaraj and Mrs. Gandhi vie for the designation, "best qualified," with the former having a slight edge, 26 to 21 and 22 to 17, in the pairs ranking. Chavan is clearly third choice and Desai the weakest in this Q. The over-all élite preference was for cooperation between Congress President and Prime Minister.

Once more the MP component in Kamaraj's Rank 1 rating is disproportionately low (30 per cent of the total actual MP respondents and 42 per cent of the total actual respondents from all groups). For Mrs. Gandhi, the weightage of MPs is much higher (46 and 35 per cent, respectively). For Chavan the proportions were almost identical. In short, *Congress MPs had greater faith in Mrs. Gandhi's ability than in Kamaraj's ability to maintain Party harmony.*

Implementation of a Socialist Program. Kamaraj emerges clearly as the person most likely to carry out a leftist program, Mrs. Gandhi second, Chavan third, and Desai last. The spread between first and second place is almost identical to the next link (10 and 11). There is little difference in Rank 1 frequency between Chavan and Desai but a very great difference between them in Rank 4. The élite rating in this Q is easily scaled but it is not too pointed.

Providing a Better Climate for Business. Here Desai is the undisputed first choice, with Mrs. Gandhi in second place; Chavan is third, and Kamaraj last. Desai's Rank 1 frequency exceeds that of the other three persons combined. Moreover, there is a substantial spread between first and second, and between second and third places. Desai is accorded a slight over-all majority.

Here the weightage of MPs' rating is heavily in favor of Desai, at the expense of Mrs. Gandhi. Desai's proportion of total actual Rank 1 frequency is 66 per cent, and his proportion of total actual MP respondents is 63 per cent. For Mrs. Gandhi, the comparable figures are 37 and 23 per cent. In this Q, then, MPs showed less trust in Mrs. Gandhi.

Ability to Solve Economic Problems. Desai's effective majority is evident in the spread. No other Congress leader competes with him in terms of over-all élite assessment. Indeed, he possesses an impressive 3 to 1 ratio in Rank 1 frequency compared to all other candidates. Stated slightly differently, the élite sample had little faith in the ability of any Congress leader except Desai to deal effectively with economic problems.

The pattern of Q 13 is reversed – *MPs preferred Desai less relatively than they did Mrs. Gandhi.* His proportion of total actual respondents in Rank 1 was 55 per cent while his Rank 1 frequency among total actual MP respondents was lower, 50 per cent. For Mrs. Gandhi, the comparable figures were 18 and 24 per cent. To a lesser extent, the MP weightage for Chavan and Kamaraj was also proportionately high.

Foreign Policy. The primacy of Mrs. Gandhi in this Q is even greater than that of Desai in the preceding one. Although the spread between her Rank 1 frequency and that of second place Desai is less than the corresponding spread in the economic realm, Mrs. Gandhi's Rank 1 frequency in Foreign Policy is greater than that of the other three persons combined. Unlike the economic Q, there is a clear second rating in Foreign Policy – Desai; the other two leaders have a distinctly inferior rating.

In this Q, too, Mrs. Gandhi has a proportionately high MP weightage (55.7 per cent of the total actual respondents of all groups and 73.5 per cent of the total actual MP respondents). For Desai, the weightage is reversed, the comparable figures being 23.5 and 15 per cent. Thus, *MPs had greater trust in Mrs. Gandhi's than in Desai's ability in the foreign policy sphere.*

SUMMARY AND ANALYTICAL THEMES

Qualities of Leadership

1. The four most important qualities initiated by the élite as a whole are Effective Leadership, Strong Leadership, Holding Congress Together, and Maintaining North-South Unity. Not one respondent considered skill in foreign policy as necessary to a Prime Minister of India in 1967. The only other quality mentioned by none was Providing a Better Climate for Business, indicating denigration of the role of private business in national growth.

2. Congress MPs stressed Strong Leadership, Effective Leadership, Maintaining North-South Unity, Intellectual Distinction, Ability to Deal with the States, and Holding Congress Together, in that order of importance. They paid scant attention to skill in handling economic problems.

3. Congress leaders displayed a wide range of emphasis, with special attention on Strong Leadership, Effective Leadership, and Holding Congress Together.

4. Defeated, Disillusioned, and Ex-Congressmen shared with Opposition leaders the primary concern with Ability to Solve Economic Problems: Two thirds of the non-Congress respondents stressed this quality, while only 7 out of 45 Congress interviewees did so.

5. Academics and Journalists revealed a pronounced pluralism in their selection of leadership qualities.

6. Stated in comparative group terms:

    a) Both sections of Congress respondents placed the greatest stress on Effective and Strong Leadership.

    b) Both sections of the Congress élite shared with the two nonpolitical groups this emphasis on Effective and Strong Leadership.

    c) The two segments of the élite diverged in their emphasis — non-Congress respondents emphasized

Ability to Solve Economic Problems, while Congress respondents stressed Effective and Strong Leadership.

d) The incumbent political élite does not appear to place a high value on economic prosperity and growth; the competing élites do.

e) One nonpolitical élite group, Indian Journalists, shared with the non-Congress political groups an emphasis on Ability to Solve Economic Problems.

Ranking of Congress Candidates

7. There was a clear preference for Mrs. Gandhi among the élite respondents as a whole. Desai was the second over-all choice; and Chavan and Kamaraj were bunched together.

8. *Mrs. Gandhi* had the most positive image within India and in the world at large. She would contribute most to the Maintenance of North-South Unity, it was believed, and is most trusted by India's minorities. She was also regarded as the most flexible Congress leader and the ablest in dealing with the states, as well as the most highly skilled in the realm of foreign policy. It is noteworthy that no single Congress leader was regarded as pre-eminent in the Ability to Deal with the States.

Mrs. Gandhi was ranked low in the qualities of Strong Leadership and Ability to Solve Economic Problems. Most respondents thought her least likely to provide Strong Leadership. Yet this quality was given overriding importance. In the Ability to Solve Economic Problems only Desai was highly rated.

9. *Morarji Desai* was ranked highest in four qualities — Effective Leadership, Strong Leadership, Providing a Better Climate for Business, and Ability to Solve Economic Problems. He was the clear but not decisive choice for most effective leadership. There was also a very broad consensus that he was the strongest personality among the four candidates.

Desai's shortcomings, in the élite view, extend to three areas: flexibility, relations with Congress leaders, and implementation of a socialist program.

10. *Kamaraj* ranked well in Holding Congress Together, but the data reflected a widely shared and widely expressed view that no single Congress leader could keep the party together; cooperation among the four is required. The same image applied to Harmony among the Party leaders. Among the four Congress candidates, Kamaraj was regarded as the most likely to implement the Congress commitment to socialism, if he were in power; but only a minority of respondents thought that even he would do so.

    Kamaraj was regarded as the least effective of the four Congress leaders, the least qualified to deal with the Opposition in Parliament and with the states, the least capable of Providing a Better Climate for Business, and the least competent in Foreign Policy.

11. *Chavan* was not ranked the highest in any sphere, and he was rated the least qualified in four; thus his over-all standing in the élite assessment is lowest among the four Congress leaders. He was regarded as having the weakest National Image and International Image — the least known and least respected Congress leader on the world stage. Chavan was also ranked the least effective of the four in terms of the goal of Congress unity, but all four are individually weak in this respect. Finally, Chavan was perceived as the least-trusted by India's minorities, a spill-over from his image as a "Maharashtrian parochialist."

12. *Congress MPs* rated Desai more favorably than Mrs. Gandhi in National Image. They had greater faith than Others in the ability of Mrs. Gandhi and Desai to Hold Congress Together, even more than in Kamaraj. They were less impressed with Desai's qualifications as a Strong Leader than were Others. In her Ability to Deal with the Opposition in Parliament, the proportionate influence of the MP component is very high; for Chavan, it is relatively low. Congress MPs had greater faith in Mrs.. Gandhi's Ability to Maintain Party Harmony

than in Kamaraj. MPs also heavily preferred Desai to Mrs. Gandhi in Ability to Provide a Better Climate for Business. In Ability to Solve Economic Problems they preferred Mrs. Gandhi. Finally, they had greater trust in her ability to conduct Foreign Policy.

Congress MPs showed a high degree of consistency in ranking the requisite qualities of an Indian Prime Minister in 1967. The most important qualities were perceived to be Effective Leadership, Strong Leadership, Holding Congress Together, and Maintaining North-South Unity (No. 2 above). As such, they articulated an overriding concern with two problems — national integration and the unity of Congress, India's pre-eminent political institution. All other issues were secondary. This evidence supports an earlier hypothesis that the Congress rank-and-file have an essentially manipulative image: The task of leadership is to preserve the unity of the polity and of the party. It is striking that Congress MPs perceive no connection between political viability and the capacity to solve economic problems. Rather, their image of national integration is linked to North-South unity and to containment of state pressures on the federal government.

This emphasis on Holding Congress Together is entirely consistent with the awareness of the impact of party factionalism on the election results. Indeed, the logical product of that image is the demand that the leadership improve the organizational performance of Congress. This reflects again a basic theme of Congress respondents — an image that is focused on political institutions rather than on public policy.

The image of Congress leaders displayed almost the same pattern (No. 3 above). It was less diffuse than that of the rank-and-file, with the greatest emphasis on Congress unity. The composite image of non-Congress respondents was strikingly different: Two thirds termed the ability to cope with India's grave economic crisis a prime requisite for the Prime Ministership; only 15 per cent of Congress respondents shared this perspective! In short, the incumbent élite, unlike competitive élites, does not appear to place a high value on economic prosperity and growth.

It was noted that not one person considered managerial skill in foreign policy necessary for the Prime Minister of India (No. 1 above). This is both expected and surprising. It is expected because of the generally low level of Congress concern with all aspects of public policy and because foreign policy is a low-priority issue in most democratic polities. It is surprising, however, in the light of the prominence of India's foreign policy in the past. The policy of "non-alignment" was defined as an extension of India's independence and gave India disproportionate influence and prestige for fifteen years. It is surprising, then, that in 1967 not one respondent considered skill in foreign policy an important quality for Prime Minister. Indeed, given India's developmental needs and its dependence on aid and trade, one would have expected this to be a significant element in the élite calculus of leadership. Viewed in a different perspective, however, the scanty attention given by the Congress respondents to economic problems is consistent with the general indifference to foreign policy.

It was also noted that the élite as a whole stressed Strong and Effective Leadership; but the component groups gave this different operational content (No. 6 above). Non-Congress respondents perceived economic problems as the most important area of public policy. The Congress rank-and-file emphasized problems of national integration and party unity. And the principal concern of Congress leaders was the continuing viability of Congress as a political party. This diversity reflects differing sets of priorities and differing images of the Indian political system as a whole. We shall return to this point in the concluding chapter.

The consistency of élite images merits notice, as they match candidates to qualities of leadership. A clear preference for Mrs. Gandhi was revealed. She ranked highest in National Image, International Image, Maintenance of North-South Unity, trust by Minorities, Flexibility, and Ability to Deal with the States (No. 8 above). Thus there is a high degree of consistency in the qualities accorded to Mrs. Gandhi and the qualities desired in a Prime Minister, especially by the Congress élite. Mrs. Gandhi's strengths are the qualities considered most important by Congress respondents. Only in one case, that of Strong Leadership, was she given a low ranking. In the crucial area of national integration, she emerged as best qualified. Not surprisingly, Mrs. Gandhi was rated weak in Ability to Solve Economic Problems; but given the relative indifference to economic problems within the Congress élite image, this deficiency was not a stumbling block to Mrs. Gandhi's re-election as Prime Minister.

Morarji Desai emerged as the clear alternative to Mrs. Gandhi, strong in areas where she is weak, and weak in areas where she exhibited her greatest strength (No. 9 above). Paradoxically, then, Desai emerges as the closest approximation to the ideal-type candidate of the Opposition. Mrs. Gandhi emerges as the closest approximation to the ideal-type candidate desired by Congress MPs and leaders. This is the setting in which images of the 1967 succession contest may now be analyzed.

CHAPTER **5**

THE SUCCESSION CONTEST: 1967

TABLE 12 : 1

CAUSES OF CHANGE IN THE ELECTION DATE FOR CONGRESS PARLIAMENTARY PARTY LEADER

ELECTION RESULTS

Question: *Do you think the decision to move forward the date of election of the Parliamentary Party Leader (from 7 April to 12 March) was influenced by the election results?*

	Congress MPs	Others	Total
Yes	20	20	40
No	13	18	31
DUAC	2	1	3
No Answer	1	5	6

OTHER CAUSES

Question: *What factors other than the election results do you think affected that decision?*

		Congress MPs	Others	Total
First	Lame Duck Session	14	14	28
	To Gain Advantage	3	2	5
	National Interest	1	1	2
	Others	8	15	23
	DUAC	9	4	13
	No Answer	1	8	9
Second	Lame Duck Session	2	4	6
	To Gain Advantage	0	3	3
	National Interest	1	1	2
	Others	0	5	5
	DUAC	8	4	12
	No Answer	25	27	52

The respondents were almost equally divided on the initial question: Forty thought there was a link between the decision to change the date for the election of the CPP Leader and the results of the General Election; 31 did not. The negative response by 44 per cent of those who replied is noteworthy — in view of the certain connection between these events. It suggests either the lack of political acumen by a high proportion of the élite sample or a reluctance to acknowledge the link — or both. The breakdown of response by groups is even more revealing.

Among the Congress rank-and-file, 20 out of 36 (55 per cent) perceived the connection; but only 4 out of 16 Congress leaders, i.e., 25 per cent, did so. In that context, the two segments of the Congress leadership responded differently: Three of the 6 Cabinet Ministers denied a connection; so did 6 of the 8 Working Committee members, who were seemingly more anxious to blur or deny the link — of which most, if not all, must have been aware. The Opposition and DDE groups were exactly equal in response. But the knowledgeable Academics and Journalists were overwhelmingly convinced of the link — 5 out of 5 and 6 out of 9, respectively. Indeed the contrast in articulated attitude of political and nonpolitical respondents is striking: Only 44 per cent of the total replies of the former were affirmative; the comparable figure among the latter was 73 per cent. In short, *the academics and communications élite members displayed a much higher awareness and acknowledgment of the link between these two important events in the succession struggle.*

There were very few elaborative comments. One very perceptive MP replied, surprisingly, "I have no opinion." An intelligent Academic concurred, "I didn't think about it." And, while one Cabinet Minister answered, "not only — or primarily" due to the election results, another said, "yes — mostly." All other replies were simply, "yes" or "no."

Various reasons were cited in response to the supplementary question about the causes of change in the date for the election of the CPP Leader; but only one attained a frequency which merits attention. This was usually designated the "Lame Duck Session."

Some respondents explained the connection; others did not; but the intent of this group was clear. It has been customary in India's political system since 1951 to hold a brief Lame Duck Session of the pre-election Lok Sabha soon after each general election in order to vote interim supplies. After a few weeks, the old Lok Sabha is dissolved, and a new Parliament, based on the election returns, is then summoned. Until 1962, the Congress held an overwhelming majority, and the re-election of Nehru as CPP Leader was a certainty; hence the holding of a Lame Duck Session was a formality, without political consequence.

In 1967, the circumstances attending the Lame Duck Session were fundamentally different. For one thing, the Congress majority in the Lok Sabha had been slashed to a bare minimum. Moreover, it was by no means certain that Mrs. Gandhi would continue as CPP Leader and, therefore, as Prime Minister. Yet the Lame Duck Session had been fixed — before the Election — for March 13. When the Election returns were in, there developed a feeling of unreality about the old Lok Sabha meeting as if nothing had changed — with its inflated, now largely rejected Congress majority. More important, Mrs. Gandhi would be Leader of the House in the Lame Duck Session, with a cloud of uncertainty — on both sides of the House — as to whether she would remain Prime Minister or be replaced shortly thereafter. It would also seem odd to have more than 22 ministers *who were defeated* sitting in Parliament as if they had been returned. This uncertainty and delay in governmental adjustment to reality would, it was felt, be bad for India in a period of grave food shortage, a crisis of confidence, economic stagnation, and general malaise. Thus, many Congressmen and others felt that the CPP Leader ought to be elected before the Lame Duck Session on March 13; and many felt that the Lame Duck Session itself should not be held. If this happened, then obviously a new CPP Leader would have to be elected before the new Lok Sabha was convened. Largely under Opposition pressure to set the Lame Duck Session aside, this is exactly what happened. This was the (often unarticulated) rationale of those who replied, "Lame Duck Session," to the supplementary question.

Of the 80 respondents, 22 fell into the "DUAC" and "no

answer" categories — much higher than the norm in these interviews. Taking 58 actual replies as the base, almost half cited "Lame Duck Session" as the principal reason for the change in date; another 6 indicated it as the second reason. "To gain advantage" was accorded a frequency of 5 as the first reason and 3 as the second; and "national interest," 2 and 2, respectively. Thus, *only the Lame Duck Session, other than the election results, received substantial recognition as a specific cause of the change in date.*

The breakdown by groups is instructive too. Of the 26 MPs who indicated at least one reason, 14, i.e., 55 per cent, selected "Lame Duck Session." The proportion among Congress leaders was only a shade higher, 58 per cent. But among all other groups in the sample the choice of reasons was much broader, with a much smaller proportion citing "Lame Duck Session" — 1 of the 3 DDE Congressmen, 1 of the 4 Opposition leaders, 1 of the 4 Academics, and 3 of the 8 Journalists. In short, *Congress respondents were much more aware than were all other élite respondents of the impending Lame Duck Session and its implications for the election of the CPP Leader.* This difference in attitude is further confirmed by the fact that 5 of the 6 persons who cited "Lame Duck Session" as the second reason for the change in date were Congressmen.

The only respondents who indicated a candidate's advantage as the most important cause of the change in date were 3 MPs and 2 Academics. In addition, 2 Congress leaders and 1 Journalist mentioned it as the second cause of change. No clear image emerges from the multiplicity of "other" reasons noted by the interviewees. Some of these may be noted in the form of comments by respondents. One MP remarked: "To avoid bitterness in the contest — the sooner the better." Another concurred with the words, "To avoid uncertainty and confusion that would weaken the Party." Other MPs conveyed the same thought: "It would give less time for manipulation," said one. An Indian Journalist conveyed the same idea: "The prestige of Congress would suffer weeks of bickering." This same theme was echoed by an Opposition leader, 3 Cabinet Ministers, a member of the Working Committee, and an Academic. As a Minister put it, "To prevent time for the Morarji group to canvass MPs." A second "other" reason noted by an MP was that

"Opposition parties wanted it earlier," i.e., wanted to abolish the Lame Duck Session, hence the need to elect a leader early. Still another MP referred to "personal considerations — which I don't want to discuss." The "national interest" theme was summed up by an MP as, "to avoid uncertainty for the country"; an Opposition leader added, "at the worst time in the country's history." The personal advantage for Mrs. Gandhi was readily acknowledged. One MP noted, "She might not fare well in the Lame Duck Session." Another referred to "requirements of strategy for the candidates to the Prime Ministership"; a third, to the "eagerness of Mrs. Gandhi to have the decision quickly." But the most telling comment in this connection came from an articulate Cabinet Minister: "The presence of the Lame Duck Session made it more rational to change the date of election, and more convenient; but the real reason was power-political." One other reason may be noted. According to a Journalist, "Congress governments in the states could ill afford a power vacuum in the center."

TABLE 12 : 2

CHANGE IN THE ELECTION DATE FOR CONGRESS
PARLIAMENTARY PARTY LEADER
DECISION-MAKERS

Question: *Who were the individuals most instrumental in making that decision?*

	Congress MPs	Others	Total
Rank 1			
Mrs. Gandhi	10	14	24
Kamaraj	7	6	13
Chavan	1	2	3
Others	5	2	7
DUAC	8	10	18
No Answer	5	10	15
Rank 2			
Mrs. Gandhi	5	2	7
Kamaraj	3	4	7
Chavan	0	5	5
Others	6	4	10
DUAC	8	9	17
No Answer	14	20	34
Rank 3			
Mrs. Gandhi	0	0	0
Kamaraj	1	2	3
Chavan	2	0	2
Others	3	1	4
DUAC	8	9	17
No Answer	22	32	54

Two aspects of the data in Table 12 : 2 merit attention; the first
is *the low response rate,* the second *the concentrated focus.* Not even
60 per cent of the persons interviewed cited one decision-maker; only
a shade over 35 per cent mentioned two individuals, and 11 per cent
indicated more than two. Taking the "DUAC" and "no answer"
categories together, the MPs emerge as more responsive than do
Others: In Rank 1, the comparable figures are 64 and 54 per cent
response, respectively; and in Rank 2, they are 39 and 34 per cent.

The decision to change the date of election of the CPP Leader was made by the "Grand Council of the Party," comprising the Working Committee, Congress Chief Ministers, Cabinet Minister, and others. Of these 40-odd persons, two were selected by the respondents as the crucial decision-makers: Over half of those who replied (24 of the 47) selected Mrs. Gandhi as the most important, and about 30 per cent cited Kamaraj for this role. Home Minister Chavan was the only other person to receive more than one vote. In the Rank 2 category, the Prime Minister and Congress President had the same frequency, with Chavan a little less. The over-all concentration on these three leaders is evident in the fact that 61 of the 85 replies to this question designate one or another of them.

The perception of decision-makers (in this decision) is not identical among all groups in the élite sample. Congress MPs are underweighted in the over-all choice of Mrs. Gandhi as key decision-maker (28 per cent of all MPs compared to 32 per cent of all Others); they are slightly overweighted in the choice of Kamaraj. The reverse obtains in Rank 2 selection. If one combines the frequency count for Mrs. Gandhi and Kamaraj, separately, the distribution for each is equally divided between MPs and Others. Among those who replied, a higher proportion of Congress leaders designated Mrs. Gandhi in Rank 1 than did MPs (4 out of 7 compared to 10 out of 23). The greatest group concentration in favor of Mrs. Gandhi, however, was Indian Journalists (6 out of 9). Viewed in terms of *political* and *nonpolitical* respondents, a much higher proportion of the latter selected Mrs. Gandhi (8 out of 11 compared to 16 out of 35).

Others mentioned by MPs as decision-makers included Atulya Ghosh, Sanjiva Reddy, President Radhakrishnan, the Opposition, the Parliamentary Board, the entire Working Committee, and people who opposed Morarji. Members of the Working Committee added S.K. Patil and Jagjivan Ram. The essence of the decision was conveyed by a Cabinet Minister: "There was no opposition to the proposal; it was in everybody's mind, perhaps. Morarji made one observation — casual but pointed. 'If the Leader is to be someone other than the Prime Minister, would the present PM be embarrassed (if the election date is changed)?' he asked. 'No, no, I won't be,' she said."

TABLE 12 : 3

CHANGE IN THE ELECTION DATE FOR CONGRESS
PARLIAMENTARY PARTY LEADER

EFFECTS ON CANDIDATES' PROSPECTS

Question: *Do you think that this decision increased the chances of any particular candidate for the Prime Ministership?*
(To those who answered, "yes," the further questions were posed,
"whose" and "how.")

	Congress MPs	Others	Total
Yes	12	15	27
No	22	21	43
DUAC	2	3	5
No Answer	0	5	5
Yes			
Mrs. Gandhi	11	15	26
Morarji Desai	1	0	1
DUAC	0	0	0
No Answer	0	0	0
Yes			
Less Time	5	6	11
DUAC	6	7	13
No Answer	1	2	3

The evidence in Table 12:3 reveals that barely one third of the
élite sample perceived – or acknowledged – a link between the
change in date for the election of the CPP Leader and the outcome
of the succession contest; over half the respondents answered clearly
in the negative. The weight of MPs and Others in the affirmative vote
was almost identical. But the further breakdown by groups reveals
shades of difference. The affirmative vote by Congress leaders was

less than the over-all average, only 25 per cent, while both nonpolitical groups were well above the average: Academics, 50 per cent, and Journalists, 44 per cent. The combined Opposition and DDE positive replies were about 35 per cent.

The most striking fact about this data is that *all but 1 of the 27 who indicated a link identified the electoral benefit with Mrs. Gandhi.* All groups in the sample were represented in this distribution. No less noteworthy is *the focus on one reason* in reply to the supplementary question, "how": Eleven of the 27 indicated, in a variety of formulations, that *the change in date meant less time for Desai and his supporters to canvass for votes,* especially among the 105 new MPs. The distribution in this reply was proportionate, i.e., it comprised half or slightly less than half the number in each of the groups indicating Mrs. Gandhi as the beneficiary.

Among those who replied in the affirmative, almost a third elaborated with comments of substance. One MP remarked: "She was in a position of leadership and was able to maintain contact with the Chief Ministers who supported her." Another declared: "More time would have created more controversy and more doubt in her leadership." One Cabinet Minister observed: "It only reduced the period of agony." Another was more pointed: "It (the decision about the election date) was the first test; it showed she could have her way; failure would have made a difference in the outcome." One of the Academics introduced another variable: "A lapse of time would have brought a third candidate – and in that case she would have lost votes." A second added, "No one had time to canvass for strength, and she was the obvious first choice." A Journalist mentioned still another theme: "Morarji would have had more time to organize, and Kamaraj and others might have manipulated votes in Morarji's favor." Finally, in the uncharitable words of another commentator, "The Lame Duck Session would have torn the lady to bits."

TABLE 12 : 4

CHANGE IN THE ELECTION DATE FOR CONGRESS
PARLIAMENTARY PARTY LEADER

EFFECTS ON GROUP INFLUENCE WITHIN CONGRESS

Question: *Did this decision affect the relative influence of groups (like State
Chief Ministers, Parliamentary Party, Working Committee) in the
choice of the Prime Minister?*
(To those who answered, "yes," the further question was posed,
"Comment briefly on whose and how.")

	Congress MPs	Others	Total
Yes With No Further Reply	0	3	3
Yes With Further Reply	5	9	14
No	29	23	52
DUAC	1	3	4
No Answer	1	6	7

A rather small proportion of respondents perceived — or
acknowledged — a link between the change in date for the leadership
contest and the balance of influence within the Congress relating to
its outcome: Barely 20 per cent of the total sample replied in the
affirmative, and the ratio of "yes" to "no" answers was 1 to 3.

The MP component in the affirmative replies was disproportionately low (14 per cent of all MP respondents compared to 27
per cent of all Others in the "yes" category); the difference is
accentuated if one excludes the "DUAC" and "no answer"
categories, in which there is a rather high component of Others. Put
in absolute terms, only 5 of the 36 MPs indicated a link, whereas 12
of the 42 Others did so. *This suggests a lesser degree of sophistication
— or more effective concealment — among the Congress rank-and-
file. Congress leaders,* as might be expected, showed greater
awareness (5 out of 16); the *nonpolitical* respondents were slightly

less so (4 out of 15). *On the whole,* however, *the élite sample did not attribute importance to the change in date of the CPP Leader's election, either in terms of the effect on candidates' prospects* (Table 12 : 3) *or the effect on the influence of institutional interest groups within Congress* (Table 12 : 4).

Despite the paucity of affirmative replies, there were many elaborative comments of interest. One MP remarked: "It strengthened the role of Hindi Chief Ministers, plus their allies in Andhra Pradesh, Madhya Pradesh, Mysore, and Maharashtra." Another declared: "The Chief Ministers gained; they could organize their machinery quickly." While concurring in part, a third MP said: "It strengthened the Parliamentary Party — because the President and the Working Committee had to operate in a brief period of time." A Cabinet Minister also saw the CPP as the beneficiary, for "outside influences would be greater if Morarji had more time to organize." Still another MP claimed that the Chief Ministers' influence declined, because "they were pre-occupied with their own State's affairs in the early days and did not have time to organize." And one MP perceived no influence on MPs' thinking: "They would decide on individual merit and the good of the organization."

One Working Committee member stressed the Prime Minister's influence through patronage: "She could offer inducements to people. Her friends, if not she, made use of this." Another echoed the view that the Chief Ministers gained most: "It gave them a greater advantage in influencing MPs before they came to Delhi and began to think for themselves." One of the Journalists dissented: "The Chief Ministers would have played a bigger role (so too would business) if the decision had been delayed." Another saw the Working Committee as the main beneficiary: "It gave the party bosses time to organize — it was the first tactical battle." One Academic was candid in admitting: "I don't know; it would be relevant, but how is unclear." Another took a unique position: "It prevented anyone from exercising a decisive influence." Most striking, perhaps, *these comments reveal variety and independence of thought and expression among the Indian élite respondents.*

TABLE 13

MRS. GANDHI'S SELECTION IN 1966:
TENTATIVE OR NOT?

Question: *Did you think, at the time of Mrs. Gandhi's succession to Shastri,*
           that it was a tentative choice made for the period until after the
           General Election?
           (The further question was asked, "Can you specify why you thought
           so? ")

	Congress MPs	Others	Total
Yes	14	16	30
No	19	24	43
DUAC	2	1	3
No Answer	1	3	4

According to the evidence in Table 13, more than half the
respondents thought of Mrs. Gandhi as a long-term Prime Minister
when she was initially selected in 1966. Yet it is perhaps more
revealing that in the immediate aftermath of her re-election as PM in
March, 1967, no less than 30 persons, i.e., 37.5 per cent of the élite
sample indicated that they had viewed her succession to Shastri as a
tentative choice — until after the General Election. *This response*
illuminates the reality of freedom of thought and expression within
the Indian élite; there was a total absence of fear among the persons
interviewed in conveying dissent or criticism of their newly re-elected
leader.

The weight of Congress MPs and Others in the over-all "tentative
choice" frequency is almost identical (39 per cent of all MP replies
and 37 per cent of all Others); so too in the over-all "long-term
choice" frequency. The ratio in Working Committee replies is the
same (3 out of 8), but Cabinet Ministers expressed a disproportionate
loyalty to Mrs. Gandhi (1 of the 6 in "tentative choice"). The
nonpolitical groups were divided in their opinions: Academics

offered an equal distribution to the choices, 3 and 3, whereas twice as many Journalists indicated a "long-term choice" of Mrs. Gandhi (6 of the 9). As might be expected, 4 of the 5 Opposition leaders who replied viewed her selection in 1966 as tentative. In terms of *political* and *nonpolitical* respondents, the former weighed more heavily in the direction of "tentative choice" (3 to 4 and 2 to 3, respectively).

Many respondents clarified the rationale of their choice. These may be set down within each group.

MPs (Long-Term Choice)

"Once she held the chair, she would continue in the post."

"There was a contest for the post of PM — and one does not have an election for a tentative choice."

"She was the only person who could hold the Party and Government together."

"She had an overwhelming majority in 1966, and I did not think the balance of power within the Party would change." (This was the realism of a Morarji supporter.)

"Because we had full faith in her capacity to lead; she was young and had the attributes of leadership."

"We wanted continuity."

"No other leader was available."

(Tentative Choice)

"Because Kamaraj told everybody, 'I selected her because I wanted to win the elections'."

"Because she lacked the qualities required for leadership."

"Because four or five powerful members of the Parliamentary Board were able to dominate the decision."

There were about five MPs who termed it a tentative choice subject to performance:

"She was on trial," said one. "It was a probationary year," said another. "We wanted to see how she would function" or "We didn't know how she would shape up," said others.

The two opposite extremes of MP opinion were summed up as follows: "No one thought she should be a stop-gap choice"; and "At that time the Leader was elected for one year only — it was obvious."

Cabinet Ministers (Long-Term Choice)

"You don't elect a leader of a country this size for one year; besides the leader in the elections would be expected to carry on."

"She was so obviously the only person on the horizon."

"It is not in the interests of the country to change the PM."

Working Committee (Long-Term Choice)

"There was no reason to think it would be interrupted soon."

"I thought she would be amenable to collective leadership — but she acted contrary to it."

"Because she had great support, youth and good background."

"When you elect a leader, you should give him time to prove his mettle; one year is too short."

One Working Committee member conveyed the essential truth: "No thought was given to it — except to win the elections and to keep Morarji out."

Academics (Long-Term Choice)

"Whoever got in as Prime Minister would be hard to dislodge." (Another echoed this view.)

"Once elected, a Prime Minister cannot be thrown out — it is not in accord with Indian culture."

(Tentative Choice)

"I thought the Congress bosses felt so — and they were influential."

"The choice was quite a surprise."

Journalists (Long-Term Choice)

"After Nehru there was no other national leader."

"I thought of her election in 1966 as an expression of a definite and overwhelming vote of confidence."

"She had youth and seemed to have drive and a new approach."

"She had youth and Nehru's charisma."

"The isolation of Morarji made it seem a long-term choice."

(Tentative Choice)

"It was not ever meant to be a long-term choice."

Two Journalists took the position: "It was really an open issue at the time; it depended on her performance."

TABLE 14

OPINIONS AS TO THE ROLE OF CONGRESS AGENCIES IN SELECTING
THE PRIME MINISTER

Question: *Which of the following Congress agencies should participate in the de facto choice of the Prime Minister?*

		Congress MPs	Others	Total
CPP Executive				
	Yes	1	1	2
	No	35	37	72
CPP				
	Yes	35	34	69
	No	1	4	5
Working Committee				
	Yes	7	9	16
	No	29	29	58
Congress President				
	Yes	6	8	14
	No	30	30	60
Chief Ministers				
	Yes	2	4	6
	No	34	34	68
Pradesh Congress Committee Leaders	Yes	0	3	3
	No	36	35	71

Note: There were 6 in the "no answer" category—the identical persons throughout; they comprised 1 each from Cabinet, Working Committee, Chief Ministers, and Foreign Journalists, and 2 from the Opposition.

The evidence in Table 14 points to an *overwhelming consensus*: It is the members of the *Congress Parliamentary Party* who should play the *pre-eminent role* in choosing the Prime Minister; the *CPP Executive* and *Pradesh Congress Committee (PCC) leaders* and the *Chief Ministers* should play *virtually no role*; and the *Working Committee* and *Congress President* should play a *subsidiary role* in the process.

On the Parliamentary Party's legitimate role there is virtually no dissent — only 1 MP and interestingly 3 Journalists. At the other extreme, there is near-unanimity that the CPP Executive, PCC leaders, and the Chief Ministers should be excluded from the process. In the case of the first, only 1 MP and 1 Working Committee member opted for its inclusion; in the second, 1 each from the Working Committee, Academics, and Journalists, and in the third, a slightly larger number (6) — 2 MPs and 1 each from Cabinet, Working Committee, Academics, and Journalists. Noteworthy here is the attitude to Chief Ministers' participation, especially in the light of widespread knowledge that, in both the 1966 and 1967 succession contests, the Congress governmental leaders in the states did in fact play a very important role; moreover, many MPs owed their tickets to their Chief Minister. The exclusion of the CPP Executive and the PCC (state organization) leaders is not surprising, for they were of no consequence in all three succession contests.

The all-India organizational leaders, by contrast, are regarded as legitimate participants in the selection process by about 20 per cent of the actual respondents. And in both categories, Working Committee and Congress President, the weight of MPs and Others is about the same. In this context, perhaps the most striking fact is that only 2 of the 8 Working Committee members themselves claimed a legitimate role for the Committee in the *de facto* selection of the Prime Minister — this despite the fact that the Working Committee has long regarded itself as the summit of authority in the Congress on all policy and important matters. Those who granted a legitimate role to Working Committee and Congress President are widely distributed — they are represented in all groups of respondents except Opposition leaders.

Comments on this question were brief but revealing. Among the

MPs, there was near-unanimity that the CPP should play the pivotal role; all but one so indicated. Moreover, twenty MPs stressed that the choice should be exclusively reserved to the CPP — by using the word "alone" in their reply or some other clarification — "nobody else should play a role" or "just as in the U.K." or "I resent any interference" or "obviously"; two narrowed it even further — "only members of the Lok Sabha." Almost every other combination was mentioned, i.e., CPP in consultation with the Working Committee or the Congress President or the Chief Ministers or all those and the Parliamentary Board; the most frequent of these combinations (5) was the CPP in consultation with the Working Committee and the Congress President, but it was invariably added that final choice should rest with the Parliamentary Party.

All Cabinet Ministers concurred on the key role of the CPP; indeed, all but one viewed it as an exclusive role; the dissenter suggested consultation with the Working Committee, Congress President, and Chief Ministers. Three Working Commitee members agreed on the exclusive role of the CPP but, as one might expect, they showed the greatest dissent. One remarked, "Ultimately, it is the CPP right to choose, but the candidate must be acceptable to all party segments, thus the President, PCCs, and Chief Ministers come into play." Another declared in a similar vein, "All groups in the party should be consulted because it affects the whole national life and the Party's well-being." One member summed up the general élite sample view: "Others may advise, but ultimately the Parliamentary Party must have the total and complete voice; otherwise democracy is in danger." The Opposition leaders stressed the role of the Parliamentary Party. All agreed on this, some citing the U.K. model; only 2 suggested the need to consult other agencies, without specifying them. The Academics were equally divided, 3 in favor of exclusive CPP election and 3 recommending consultation with other agencies. One invoked the federalist principle: "In a federal system, acceptability by all these agencies is necessary." The Journalists did not dissent from the general emphasis on the CPP role but they added some novelties. One recommended consultation with the AICC "because it gives MPs their tickets." Another wanted to leave it exclusively to the Working Committee — "the only agency of the

Party in touch with the rank-and-file." A third suggested selection by the Grand Council of the Party.

The dominant theme of élite opinion in this matter, however, remains the consensus that *the CPP should play the pre-eminent role in the selection of the Prime Minister (when Congress has a majority in Parliament).*

The aggregate data about the selection of India's Prime Minister in 1964, 1966, and 1967 reveal clear traits in the perception of the élite sample.

The Congress President was the overwhelming choice as the most influential person or agency in all three succession contests.

No other person or Congress body was accorded a prominent role in the 1964 struggle; only the Working Commitee received a Rank 1 frequency of more than 1 and a total occurrence of 7. It should be added, however, that many respondents indicated a close interlinking of Congress President and Working Committee in their image of decision-making. (It is noteworthy that this predominant image, as articulated, is partly incorrect, for the Syndicate of Congress leaders — Atulya Ghosh, S.K. Patil, Sanjiva Reddy, and S. Nijalingappa, apart from Kamaraj — played a very important role in selecting Shastri as Prime Minister in 1964.)[1]

In the 1966 decision process, the Chief Ministers were (correctly) cited as second in importance to the Congress President; their Rank 2 frequency of 19 stands out almost as much as the Rank 1 frequency for the Congress President.

---

[1] See the author's *Nehru's Mantle; The Politics of Succession in India* (New York: Frederick A. Praeger, 1966), chaps. iii and iv.

TABLE 15 : 1

OPINIONS AS TO THE ROLE OF AGENCIES AND INDIVIDUALS IN SELECTING THE PRIME MINISTER IN 1967

Question: *Which agency(ies) or person(s) played the crucial role(s) in the selection of the Prime Minister on this occasion?* [a]

		Congress MPs	Others	Total
CPP				
	Rank 1	12	5	17
	2	0	3	3
	3	8	1	9
Working Committee				
	Rank 1	2	5	7
	2	4	4	8
	3	4	1	5
Congress President				
	Rank 1	13	16	29
	2	11	6	17
	3	4	4	8
Chief Ministers				
	Rank 1	9	5	14
	2	9	10	19
	3	9	9	18
Syndicate				
	Rank 1	0	1	1
	2	0	3	3
	3	2	0	2
Others				
	Rank 1	0	5	5
	2	10	16	26
	3	1	6	7
No Replies				
	Rank 1	0	7	7
	2	2	2	4
	3	8	23	31

[a] A few respondents explicitly ranked agencies or persons 1, 2, and 3 in importance. Most were imprecise; for example, "the Congress President, with the Working Committee and the Chief Ministers." This was ranked by the writer: Congress President 1, Working Committee 2, Chief Ministers 3. In general, Rank 1 is the most precise and reliable.

TABLE 15 : 2

OPINIONS AS TO THE ROLE OF AGENCIES AND INDIVIDUALS IN
SELECTING THE PRIME MINISTER IN 1964 AND 1966

Question: *Which agency(ies) or person(s) played the cruicial role(s) in the
succession contest of 1964 and 1966?*

		Congress MPs	Others	Total[a]
1964				
Working Committee				
	Rank 1	0	4	4
	2	1	2	3
	3	0	0	0
Congress President				
	Rank 1	4	21	25
	2	0	2	2
	3	0	1	1
Chief Ministers				
	Rank 1	0	1	1
	2	0	3	3
	3	0	0	0
1966				
CPP				
	Rank 1	0	1	1
	2	0	1	1
	3	1	1	2
Congress President				
	Rank 1	4	22	26
	2	0	4	4
	3	0	0	0
Chief Ministers				
	Rank 1	0	4	4
	2	4	15	19
	3	0	1	1

[a] All other agencies listed in Table 15 : 1 have been omitted here because of
the very high "DUAC" and "no answer" content. Thus, in 1964, the CPP
had 73 in these categories, the Syndicate was not mentioned; in 1966, the
Working Committee had 73, and the Syndicate was not mentioned. All
other figures fall in the categories of "others" and "no replies."

The *third contest,* too, was, on the whole, accurately assessed by the respondents: *Three agencies were given prominent ranking* – the Congress President, as noted, the CPP, and the Chief Ministers. While the Parliamentary Party had a slight edge in Rank 1 frequency (17 to 14), the over-all frequency gives the state governmental leaders an unchallenged claim to second place in the élite sample image of the decision process in 1967; indeed, it is just a shade less than the over-all frequency for the Congress President (51 to 54). The decline of the Working Committee and the Syndicate, following the defeat of many Congress organizational leaders, is reflected in the data of Table 15:1.[2]

The paucity of figures dealing with the 1964 and 1966 contests is due mainly to the almost total "DUAC" or "no answer" character of MP respondents; many did not have an opportunity to reply because there was insufficient time to probe all questions in interviews with MPs – and this one was often sacrificed. Perhaps the Working Committee and the Syndicate would have been accorded greater importance by the MPs; but it is highly unlikely, from other internal evidence, that the pre-eminence of the Congress President in the 1964 contest, and of the Congress President and the Chief Ministers in the 1966 contest would have been altered.

The analysis of the same data by groups of respondents adds further insight into the articulated perception of the élite sample.

The replies of MPs concerning the 1964 and 1966 contests may be ignored as too few to permit comment.

In the 1964 data there was a total Rank 1 frequency of 36, comprising the 30 indicated in Table 15:2 and 6 Others; 5 of the total were recorded by MPs. Thus, of the 31 Rank 1 ratings attributed to non-MP respondents, *21 or two thirds selected the Congress President.* More specifically, 4 out of 6 Cabinet Ministers gave Kamaraj Rank 1, as did 2 out of 6 members of the Working Committee, all 3 DDE MPs, 3 out of 5 Opposition leaders, 5 out of 7 Academics, and 3 out of 4 Journalists.

The 4 Rank 1 occurrences for the Working Committee were distributed equally among the Cabinet Ministers, Working Committee members, Opposition leaders, and Academics.

[2]See the author's "Succession in India 1967: The Routinization of Political Change," in *Asian Survey,* Vol. VII, No. 7 (July, 1967), pp. 423-43.

*A very similar pattern of Rank 1 distribution is evident in the
1966 data.* The total number of occurrences is 37, comprising the 31
indicated in Table 15:2, along with 1 for the Working Committee
and 5 Others; of the total, 5 are MPs. Thus, of the 32 Rank 1 ratings
attributed to non-MP respondents, 22 or two thirds selected the
Congress President. More specifically, this consisted of 4 of 5 Cabinet
Ministers, 4 of 7 Working Committee members, all 3 DDE MPs, 2 out
of 4 Opposition leaders, all 6 Academics, and 3 out of 5 Journalists.

*The major change from the 1964 to the 1966 data is the very
high Rank 2 frequency for the Chief Ministers.* Of the total 27
occurrences (which include 2 for the PCCs and 1 Other), 4 were from
MPs. Of the 23 non-MP respondents, 15 or two thirds cited the Chief
Ministers. More specifically, these comprised all 4 Cabinet Ministers,
2 of the 3 Working Committee members, 2 of the 3 DDE MPs, 2 of
the 4 Opposition leaders, 4 of the 5 Academics, and 1 of the 3
Journalists.

In assessing *the most influential role during the 1967 contest* for
the Prime Ministership, *MPs were almost equally divided* – 13 citing
the Congress President, 12 the CPP, and 9 the Chief Ministers. In
fact, they tended, in the manner of their articulated response, to give
all three equal weight, with a resulting diminution of the Congress
President's previous undisputed primacy. Moreover, in citing the
Chief Ministers, they invariably made it clear that they were referring
to the four key state leaders – Mishra of Madhya Pradesh, Gupta of
UP, B. Reddy of Andhra, and Nijalingappa of Mysore, especially the
first two. *Striking here is the elevation of the Parliamentary Party to
a position of prominence in the decision-making process,* another
marked change from 1964 and 1966.

The assessment by *Others* of the crucial role in the 1967 contest
reveals a very different pattern. *Only the Congress President was
accorded Rank 1 frequency by a substantial number of respondents.*
In fact, his total frequency (16) equalled the occurrences for all 4
other specific agencies combined; none received more than 5.

Viewed in lateral terms, the MP component of the Rank 1
frequency for Congress President in 1967 is slightly less than that of

Others (36 per cent of all MP replies and 43 per cent of all Others' replies). The comparable figures for both CPP and Chief Ministers' Rank 1 frequency reveal a sharp contrast: In the CPP case, as might be expected, the proportions are one third of MP replies and 14 per cent of Others' replies; and for the Chief Ministers, they are 25 and 14 per cent. In short, *many more MPs than Others attached greater importance to the role of the CPP and the Chief Ministers in the 1967 contest.*

In terms *of distribution of Rank 1 occurrences by Others,* the *CPP* received 2 each from Cabinet Ministers and Academics, and 1 from a DDE MP. The *Chief Ministers* received 3 from Journalists and 1 each from the Working Committee and Academics. The *Congress President,* by contrast, was represented in all groups of respondents: 1 of 5 Cabinet Ministers, 4 of 6 Working Committee members, 2 of 4 DDE MPs, 2 of 5 Opposition leaders, 1 of 6 Academics, and 6 of 9 Journalists.

In the Rank 2 frequency for the 1967 contest, the weight of MPs and Others is reversed: 0 to 3 (rather than 12 to 5) for the CPP, 11 to 6 (rather than 13 to 16) for the Congress President, and 9 to 10 (rather than 9 to 5) for the Chief Ministers. It is noteworthy, too, that the Rank 2 occurrences for the Chief Ministers are greater than for the CPP and Congress President combined. The occurrences for the Chief Ministers are divided: 3 each from Cabinet Ministers and Academics, 2 from Journalists, and 1 each from DDE MPs and the Opposition. For the Congress President, there are 2 each from Academics and Journalists, and 1 each from Cabinet and Working Commitee.

The *most striking point about the Rank 3 distribution in 1967 is the high frequency for the Chief Ministers* — 18 compared to 24 for all other specific agencies combined. The 18 are equally divided between MPs and Others, with 3 from the Working Committee, 2 each from Academics and Journalists, and 1 each from DDE MPs and the Opposition.

The most significant conclusion about the image of the 1967 contest is that the élite respondents perceived the decision as a product of 3 agencies — Congress President, CPP, and Chief Ministers. The last acquires added recognition from the specific selection

of C.B. Gupta and D.P. Mishra as most influential by 2 persons.
(Gupta was also given Rank 2 by 7 other persons, and Mishra by 2.)
Rank 1 was also given to Mrs. Gandhi, Asoka Mehta, and the
"Business Community."

TABLE 16

CONSISTENCY OF CHOICE OF PRIME MINISTER

Question: *Which candidate did you support immediately after the General
Election?*

	Congress MPs	Others	Total
Mrs. Gandhi	22	20	42
Morarji Desai	9	6	15
Others	1	3	4
DUAC	0	7	7
No Answer	4	8	12

Question: *Did you support the same candidate at the time of the CPP meeting
to elect the Prime Minister?*

Yes	30	31	61
No	2	1	3
DUAC	0	1	1
No Answer	4	11	15

Question: (To those who answered, "yes," to the above question) *Did you at
any time during the two weeks before the CPP meeting feel that
another candidate might be better?*

Yes	0	1	1
No	29	29	58
DUAC	1	0	1
No Answer	0	1	1

The 1967 succession contest was settled by a compromise agreement between the two leading candidates, Mrs. Gandhi and Morarji Desai. The latter was to be appointed Deputy Prime Minister, as well as Finance Minister; in return, he would not press for a secret ballot at the CPP leadership convention on March 12. Thus, unlike the struggle for the succession to Shastri in 1966, the actual division of support within the Parliamentary Party will never be known. It is in this context that the evidence in Table 16 assumes analytical significance.

Two propositions emerge clearly from this data. *First, Mrs. Gandhi would have secured a substantial majority in the CPP had a ballot been held immediately after the General Election – or at any time in the days thereafter, culminating in the CPP convention itself, on March 12, 1967. Secondly, the élite sample as a whole displayed a very high degree of consistency in its choice for the Prime Ministership throughout the crucial fortnight of the contest.* These propositions merit further exploration.

The right to vote in the election of the CPP Leader (who was to become the PM) was held by CPP members only. In the sample of 36 MPs, 60 per cent supported Mrs. Gandhi, while 25 per cent supported Desai. (The 1 "other" vote went to Kamaraj.) Acknowledged changes in preference during the period preceding the leadership convention were marginal. Thus it is appropriate to project these sample figures, one twelfth of the total CPP membership, to arrive at a probable distribution of the total CPP votes. The result would be as follows:

Mrs. Gandhi:	22 x 12	264
Morarji Desai:	9 x 12	108
Other and Uncertain:	5 x 12	60
	Total	432

Since 30 of the 33 clear MP choices did not change, the above projection may be "corrected" by a subtraction of one eleventh from the initial raw totals. Thus, whereas the majority for Mrs. Gandhi in the initial projection would be 264–108, i.e., *156,* the corrected majority would be 240–98, i.e., *142.* In proportional terms, Mrs.

Gandhi would have received 70 per cent of the projected totals of clear choices.

All Cabinet Ministers but 1 and some of the Working Committee members interviewed also had the right to vote as CPP members. The data reveal a 4 to 1 majority for Mrs. Gandhi within each group — further accentuating the spread in votes. It is possible that the replies, given after the contest was settled, contain biases; however, the impressive freedom of expression demonstrated in other more delicate areas of questioning after the contest, notably the ranking of leadership qualities, suggests that such bias, if it exists, would not be severe. Certainly *the validity of Proposition 1,* noted above, *seems beyond doubt.*

The distribution of choices within the 2 *Congress leadership groups* has already been noted (8 to 2 in favor of Mrs. Gandhi). The *Academics* were unanimous, 5 of 5 clear votes for Mrs. Gandhi. The *Journalists* were more evenly divided, 3 to 2, with 1 other. Desai's 15 votes were drawn from MPs (9), Journalists (2), and 1 each from Cabinet, Working Committee, DDE, and Opposition leaders.

The validity of Proposition 2 is abundantly clear from the replies to the supplementary questions. Only 3 respondents, 2 MPs and 1 Working Committee member, explicitly indicated that they had changed their preference by the time of the CPP convention; 61, by contrast, were firm. And of the 61 who remained consistent, only 1, a Journalist, wavered in the intervening two weeks. Assuming honesty and accurate recall, and there is no reason to doubt either, this strongly suggests that *the choice of PM among the élite sample was fixed at least as early as the announcement of the General Election results, probably earlier, and that the respondents were not influenced by the political battle between the contenders. They had made up their minds long before they would have been called upon to vote for a CPP Leader.*

TABLE 17

EXPECTATIONS AS TO THE RESULT OF SECRET BALLOT
(POST-OUTCOME)

Question: *Did you think that there was any question as to whether Mrs. Gandhi
would win or not?*

	Congress MPs	Others	Total
No Doubt	30	26	56
Doubt	2	9	11
DUAC	2	5	7
No Answer	2	4	6

Question: *By what majority did you think Mrs. Gandhi would win?*

	Congress MPs	Others	Total
100 or More than 100	7	15	22
More than 50 but less than 100	2	4	6
Less than 50	2	7	9
DUAC	3	4	7
No Answer	23	13	36

Question: *When did Mrs. Gandhi's victory become obvious to you?*

	Congress MPs	Others	Total
When Election Results Announced or Soon After	16	13	29
Other	9	1	10
DUAC	2	0	2
No Answer	9	30	39

Further insight into élite perceptions of the 1967 succession
contest may be acquired from the data in Table 17. *A substantial
majority* of all respondents (70 per cent) and an overwhelming
majority of those who gave clear replies (83.5 per cent) *expressed no
doubt as to the outcome of a secret ballot.* The doubters were few in
number but they were widely represented: 2 MPs, 3 Congress leaders,
1 each from the DDE, Opposition, and Academic groups, and 3

Journalists. In group ratio terms, however, the nondoubters held great margins (15 to 1 for MPs, 11 to 3 for Congress leaders, 5 to 1 for Academics, etc.); the only exception was Journalists, 4 to 3 in favor of nondoubters.

The evidence is also revealing on the question of likely majority for Mrs. Gandhi. The projections based on the data in Table 16 indicated a majority ranging from 156 to 142. The élite sample seems to agree. Of the 37 clear replies, 22 (60 per cent) estimated a majority of 100 or more; almost 80 per cent predicted a majority of more than 50. Of some interest in this context is the breakdown by groups. The weight of MPs in the over-all frequency of "100 or more" is much less than that of Others, but that is simply due to the fact that two thirds of MP respondents gave no reply. More relevant, 8 of the 10 Congress leaders who replied fell within the "100 or more" group; Cabinet Ministers ranked higher than Working Committee · members in this respect. In all other groups, the distribution was relatively even — except for Journalists: Three estimated a majority of 100 or more, and 2 others at least 50. The central point, however, is *the widely distributed expectation of a CPP majority of 100 or more for Mrs. Gandhi.*

The replies to the second supplementary question also reveal a *consensus — that, as soon as the General Election results were announced (February 25 to 27) or soon thereafter, Mrs. Gandhi's victory in the succession contest was assured;* 29 of 39 clear replies (74 per cent) so indicated. Most of the "Other" specified dates fell in the range of March 4 to 9 and were accompanied by the explanation — "after I returned to Delhi and talked with friends in the party." All but one of the non-MP respondents who replied noted the Election results as the determinant of their assessment that Mrs. Gandhi was bound to win. One MP was less than kind, with the words: "Mrs. Gandhi had already manipulated the votes." Another cited as the determinant — "when we knew that C.B. Gupta, Mishra, and Brahmananda Reddy (Chief Ministers of UP, Madhya Pradesh, and Andhra, respectively) had thrown their full weight to Mrs. Gandhi — by March 8 or 9." But these were atypical comments; most were certain earlier.

TABLE 18 : 1

COMMUNICATION AND CONSULTATION IN THE SELECTION PROCESS FOR PRIME MINISTER (1967)

Question: *Did you, before the CPP meeting, discuss your voting and/or the leadership contest with the following?*

		Congress MPs	Others[a]	Total
Other Members of CPP				
	Yes	31	7	38
	No	2	0	2
	No Answer	3	7	10
President of Your PCC				
	Yes	14	0	14
	No	19	7	26
	No Answer	3	7	10
Chief Minister of Your State				
	Yes	18	1	19
	No	15	6	21
	No Answer	3	7	10
Congress President				
	Yes	17	6	23
	No	16	1	17
	No Answer	3	7	10
Other National Leaders				
	Yes	20	7	27
	No	13	0	13
	No Answer	3	7	10

Question: *Were you a member of any group of CPP members who met formally or informally to decide on a common voting strategy?*

	Congress MPs	Others	Total
Yes	18	6	24
No	15	1	16
No Answer	3	7	10

[a] Others are confined to Cabinet Ministers and Working Committee members. Members of all other groups were excluded, for they were not members of the CPP.

The pattern of intra-Congress consultation during a major all-India political crisis is clearly revealed by the data in Table 18:1.

MPs

Almost all (31 of 36) discussed the succession contest and their voting with other members of the CPP.

Sixty per cent also discussed it with "National Leaders"; the most frequently mentioned were Atulya Ghosh, Y.B. Chavan, and Sanjiva Reddy.

Half the MPs in the sample acknowledged having consulted their Chief Minister and the Congress President.

Forty per cent saw their PCC President as well.

All this suggests *an intense, face-to-face contact between the Congress rank-and-file MPs and Congress leaders at the all-India and state levels; there is a highly integrated communication network within the majority party of India's political system.*

Congress Leaders

All 7 of the Cabinet Ministers and Working Committee members who replied acknowledged having consulted MPs and other "National Leaders."

Six of them also discussed the contest with the Congress President; indeed there is abundant evidence to show that consultation between some of these leaders and the Congress President was very intense — daily and, in the case of some, more than once a day.[3]

No less striking, only 1 of the 7 bothered to discuss the contest with the Chief Minister of his state.

Not one exchanged views with the PCC President of his state.

In short, *the gap in communication within the Congress during the succession contest would seem to have been between those who*

---

[3] Appendix C contains the Appointment Diary of Congress President Kamaraj during the succession struggle of 1967, from February 26 to March 12.

considered themselves all-India leaders and the state leaders, governmental and organizational, from the states from which they originally came. These "National Leaders" did consult a few, select Chief Ministers, like Mishra, Gupta, Nijalingappa, and Reddy, because of their "national" stature or their control over a large bloc of votes.

The existence of powerful pressure groups during the succession contest of 1967 is evident from other sources.[4] It is confirmed by the replies to the supplementary question in this table: Sixty per cent of the persons who replied acknowledged being active in groups of CPP members who met to influence the outcome of the contest; the proportion is higher among the Congress leaders, as one would expect, 6 of 7; but half the total MPs in the sample also indicated their involvement in group discussion and action. Indeed, the number that denied such involvement (15) is rather surprising and *suggests a not fully integrated network of communication and consultation within the Congress at an élite level.*

TABLE 18 : 2

INITIATIVE IN THE SELECTION PROCESS FOR PRIME MINISTER (1967)

Question: *Did you convene any meetings with Congress MPs or others during the two weeks before the election of the CPP leader on March 13?*

	Congress MPs	Others	Total
Yes	10	11	21
No	23	5	28
Irrelevant[a]	0	24	24
DUAC and No Answer	3	4	7

[a] This category refers to all non-Congress respondents, i.e., to the 7 Opposition leaders, the 6 Academics, and the 11 Journalists.

[4] Brecher, "Succession in India 1967," pp. 423-43.

It was noted from the data in Table 18:1 that Congress is characterized by an intense and highly (though not fully) integrated network of communication at the all-India and state levels. The pattern of initiative is rather different, however. Among the sample of 80 respondents, 31 may be disregarded here: the 24 Irrelevant, the 4 DDE MPs, who are in the DUAC and No Answer category, and 3 MPs who did not reply. Of the 49 clear answers, 57 per cent indicated that they did not convene meetings during the 1967 contest, while 43 per cent acknowledged having done so. But these are aggregate figures; the breakdown by groups is more revealing.

Barely one fourth (10) of the 36 Congress MPs acknowledged that they had taken the initiative to bring colleagues together to help shape the outcome of the contest; almost two thirds (23) declared that they had not done so. The contrast with the pattern of communication is striking: Over 80 per cent had admitted to some form of consultation with fellow MPs, and half had spoken to the Congress President, as well as their Chief Minister and PCC leader. In short, as might be expected, *the Congress MPs as a group were the objects of courting and attention during the 1967 contest, rather than initiators of political action. Initiative lay with the party leaders:* Eleven of the 16 stated that they had convened meetings – 5 of 6 Cabinet Ministers, 5 of 8 Working Committee members, and 1 of the Chief Ministers.

This is by no means a complete list of those who took the initiative during the contest; there were others not included in the sample. Perhaps double the number of Others would be an accurate estimate. This would suggest the conclusion that, of the 500-odd Congress MPs and organizational leaders, Chief Ministers, etc., *about 6 per cent took initiatives during the struggle* over who should be the CPP Leader and therefore the Prime Minister.

TABLE 19 : 1

ELITE ATTITUDES TO THE NEW CABINET (MARCH, 1967)

Questions: *Were you satisfied or dissatisfied with the manner in which the new*
Cabinet was formed?

Do you regard the composition of the new Cabinet as impressive or
acceptable or unimpressive or unacceptable?

	Congress MPs	Others	Total
Manner of Formation			
Satisfied With	7	14	21
Dissatisfied With	8	7	15
No Answer or DUAC[a]	21	23	44
Composition			
Acceptable or Impressive	7	12	19
Unacceptable or Unimpressive	7	9	16
No Answer[a]	22	23	45

[a] The large number of respondents in this category is due to two reasons:
First, most of the Congress MPs were interviewed before the Cabinet was
announced, and there was no opportunity to go back to those persons;
and secondly, these questions were not in the original questionnaire and
were invariably asked at the end of the interview — when time permitted.
Almost all "no answer" figures are to be explained by these factors and
may be disregarded.

The data in Table 19:1 (as well as in Table 19:2) are not as rich
in one respect as those in almost all preceding tables — for reasons
indicated in the preceding explanatory note. The paucity of clear
Congress MP replies virtually eliminates that category, 45 per cent of
the total replies, from meaningful analysis. Nevertheless, the

attitudes and opinions of the Other respondents can be explored.

Almost half of those persons provided clear replies. In the *aggregate* the ratio of those who were satisfied with the *manner* of the Cabinet's formation to those who were dissatisfied was 2 to 1; the comparable ratio concerning the *composition* of Cabinet was less, only 1.3 to 1. In *group* terms, those meriting attention are Cabinet Ministers, Academics, and Journalists. Whereas the *Working Committee members, DDE MPs* — and even those *Congress MPs* canvassed — *were split* on the manner of Cabinet formation, 1 to 1, 1 to 1, and 7 to 8, respectively, those three groups showed sharper divisions of response: Three of 4 Cabinet Ministers were satisfied, as were 5 of 6 Academics; but only 2 of 5 Journalists expressed satisfaction. Indicative, too, of different intellectual interests, all 6 Academics gave clear replies, but only 5 of 9 Journalists did so — though all were asked this question. On the matter of composition, again the *Working Committee members, DDE MPs,* and *Congress MPs were split* — 1 to 1, 1 to 1, and 7 to 7, respectively; so too were Opposition leaders, 1 to 1; Cabinet Ministers followed the earlier division — 4 termed it acceptable, 2 did not. But both nonpolitical groups reversed their attitude: Only 2 of 6 Academics found the Cabinet composition acceptable, while 3 of 5 Journalists did so.

Some of the elaborative comments are worth noting in this context. Among the Congress MPs, one expressed his displeasure by saying, "Morarji's people were kept out." Further, there was the prediction that internal friction may develop, because "Morarji is loyal but is firm in policies; for him the nation comes first." Another MP concurred: "It was right to bring Morarji into the Cabinet — but others of his group should have been included." A third MP, by contrast, remarked: "I don't think I am unhappy with the Cabinet; it will accelerate the role of decision-making by the CPP." Still another was bluntly critical: "Mrs. Gandhi's Cabinet consists of yes-men." And finally, the theme of unequal representation was aired by an MP: "It would have been better if all sections of the party, society and country would have been represented."

The view of Mrs. Gandhi's camp was expressed by a Cabinet Minister: "To have a weakened Morarji in the Cabinet is one thing; to have two conflicting groups is another." Congress President Kamaraj recalled that the Prime Minister had shown him the list before it was announced: "I told her, 'whatever you want'." He made no comment as to whether Desai's supporters were excluded in toto from the Cabinet. Another organizational leader declared: "There is a terrific amount of discontent among the 280 (Congress) MPs; she has packed the Cabinet with her own people." According to one of the DDE MPs, however, "She had her own mind and took her own decisions; she consulted only those she wanted to — which is as it should be." His only criticism was the canvassing for ministerial posts by eager aspirants and the excessive size of the Cabinet.

One Academic perceived that, while the manner of formation was "alright," the Cabinet's composition "reflected neither the complexion of the Party nor a Cabinet of talent." Another was more blunt in his criticism: "Indira, with a vengeance, made a Cabinet that was hers — to prove it to the world. If the formula (to bring Desai into the Cabinet) had been arrived at without intervention, a more composite Cabinet would have ensued. Morarji will be loyal and dignified." A third Academic was disdainful: "I am not disappointed with its composition — there is not much to choose from." And a fourth was more sanguine: "It was done speedily, a good thing"; as to its membership, "There are some young people; Mrs. Gandhi has done better than Nehru."

Among the Journalists, one declared with concern: "Mrs. Gandhi, like Nehru, is willful; Morarji has to deal with three of her men (in economic and financial matters) — Asoka (Mehta), Dinesh (Singh), and Fakhruddin (Ali Ahmed); she created a quadrilateral, which will tear the Cabinet apart." A colleague was more sympathetic: "It is a good team but inexperienced; it is not likely to be able to deliver the goods in the present circumstances, but it will be disciplined."

The *aggregate* distribution of replies among persons other than Congress MPs to the speculative question about the probable duration of the new 1967 Government was fairly even. More noteworthy is the fact that only 5 of 27 substantive replies indicated the probability of a full 5 year term; and only 11, i.e., 40 per cent, expected the Government to last more than 2 years. The numbers are too small to suggest meaningful *group* distribution; yet 4 of 9

TABLE 19 : 2

ELITE OPINIONS AS TO PROBABLE DURATION OF THE
NEW GOVERNMENT (MARCH, 1967)

Question: *How long do you think the new Government will last, a full term
of 5 years or less?*

	Congress MPs	Others	Total
Full Term of 5 Years	3	5	8
More than 2 but less than 5 Years	1	6	7
Twelve to 24 months	2	6	8
Less than 12 Months	0	2	2
Uncertain (Don't know)	0	8	8
No Answer[a]	30	17	47

[a] See the note to Table 19 : 1.

Journalists expressed uncertainty about the Government's survival capacity for a full term, and 2 others expected the Government to fall before 24 months. Academics were more sanguine, 2 of 6 predicting a full term, and another 2 at least 2 years.

Comments are more revealing than the statistical data of this table. One Cabinet Minister declared: "The survival of Congress Government depends on what we do in the next few years. I personally feel that basic changes in policy are necessary." In any event, "I rule out military rule in the next 5 years." Another remarked: "It will all depend on the economic situation; two good monsoons and Congress will be back." This view was echoed by a defeated Congress MP and an Academic. The latter added, "The whole political system depends on the next two monsoons." An ex-Congress MP observed, about probable duration of the 1967 Government, "at the moment, 1 year; if it lasts 2 years, it could continue 5." A Journalist concurred but used "15 months" as the initial testing time. Another observed, "It is difficult to say — but who is going to bring down the Government."

One Opposition leader asserted with confidence: "It can't last 5 years — 1 year or 2; there is a 50-50 chance of chaos, followed by (I hope) military rule." Another predicted midterm elections followed by a coalition or all-Party Government.

SUMMARY AND ANALYTICAL THEMES

Date of Election of CPP Leader
  1. Academic and communications interviewees displayed a much higher awareness and acknowledgment of the link between the change in election date and the succession struggle than did Congress respondents (73 to 45 per cent). Only the "Lame Duck Session" and the General Election results received substantial recognition as specific causes of the change in date. Congressmen were much more aware than were all other élite respondents of the impending "Lame Duck Session" and its implications for the election of the CPP leader.
  2. There was a low response rate and a concentration on two persons in regard to the question of decision-makers on the change in date. Congress MPs are underweighted in the over-all choice of Mrs. Gandhi as key decision-maker, and are slightly overweighted in the choice of Kamaraj. The greatest group emphasis on Mrs. Gandhi was Indian Journalists. In general, a much higher proportion of nonpolitical respondents chose Mrs. Gandhi.
  3. Barely one third of the élite sample perceived a direct link between the change in date and *outcome* of the succession contest. All but 1 of the 27 who did so identified Mrs. Gandhi as the beneficiary. The principal reason cited was that the change in date meant less time for Desai and his supporters to canvass votes.

4. Barely one fifth of the respondents acknowledged a link between the change in date and group influence on the selection process. The Congress rank-and-file were least aware of any effect; Congress leaders were more aware. On the whole, however, the élite sample did not attribute importance to the change in date of the CPP Leader's election, either in terms of effects on candidates' prospects or the effect on the influence of institutional interest groups within Congress in determining the outcome.

Selection Process for Prime Minister

5. There was an overwhelming consensus that members of the Congress Parliamentary Party should play the dominant role in choosing the Prime Minister; that the CPP Executive, the PCC leaders, and the Chief Ministers should play virtually no role; and that the Working Committee and Congress President should play a subsidiary role.

    Noteworthy is the attitude to participation of the Chief Ministers, in the light of widespread knowledge that they were very influential in the 1966 and 1967 succession contests.

6. On the actual selection process in the three post-Nehru contests, the main themes were as follows:

    a) The Congress President was the overwhelming choice as the most influential person or agency in all three contests.

    b) No other person or Congress body was accorded a prominent role in the 1964 struggle.

    c) In the 1966 decision the Chief Ministers were (correctly) cited as second in importance to the Congress President.

    d) The Congress President, the CPP, and the Chief Ministers were correctly cited in the 1967 contest.

    e) The major change from the 1964 to the 1966 data is the very high Rank 2 frequency for the Chief Ministers.

    f) In assessing the 1967 contest, MPs were equally divided

among three institutions. Others, however, accorded Rank 1 frequency only to the Congress President. In short, many more MPs than Others attached greater importance to the role of the CPP and the Chief Ministers in the 1967 contest.

7. The élite sample as a whole displayed a very high degree of consistency in its choice for the Prime Ministership throughout the crucial fortnight of the 1967 contest. Mrs. Gandhi would have secured a substantial majority in the CPP had a secret ballot been held immediately after the Fourth General Election — or at any time in the days thereafter, culminating in the CPP convention itself. The choice of PM among the élite sample was fixed at least as early as the announcement of the General Election results; and the respondents were not influenced by the political battle between the two principal contenders, Mrs. Gandhi and Desai.

8. A substantial majority of all respondents (70 per cent) expressed no doubt as to the outcome of a secret ballot. A consensus existed that, as soon as the General Election results were announced, or soon thereafter, Mrs. Gandhi's victory in the succession contest was assured.

9. There was intense face-to-face contact between the Congress rank-and-file MPs and Congress leaders at the all-India and state levels in the 1967 contest. This revealed a highly integrated communications network within the majority party of India's political system. Almost all MPs discussed the contest with other members of the CPP, 60 per cent discussed it with National Congress Leaders, 50 per cent with their Chief Minister and the Congress President, and 40 per cent consulted their PCC President as well.

Congress leaders consulted MPs and other "National Leaders"; 6 of the 7 consulted with the Congress President as well; but only 1 talked to the Chief Minister of his state; and not 1 exchanged views with the PCC President of his state.

In short, the communication gap within the Congress during

the 1967 succession contest would seem to have been
between those who considered themselves all-India leaders
and the state leaders, both governmental and organizational,
from their home states.

The New Government

10. Cabinet Ministers and Academics were satisfied with the
    manner of Cabinet formation and its composition. Journal-
    ists were not. All other groups of respondents were divided
    in their view.
11. Only 40 per cent of those who gave clear replies on probable
    duration expected the new government to remain in office
    more than two years.

Indian élite images of the mechanics of choosing a Prime
Minister varied considerably in awareness and perspicacity. As noted
(No. 1 above), only 55 per cent of the Congress rank-and-file
respondents perceived a link between the advancing of the date for
selection of the CPP Leader and the contest; and only 25 per cent of
the Congress leaders did so. By contrast, 73 per cent of the
communications élite acknowledged the link between these two
important events. All but one of the respondents who perceived this
connection emphasized the benefit to Mrs. Gandhi. The nonpolitical
interviewees were thus more aware of the internal political and
manipulative processes of the Congress Party. Somewhat surprisingly,
Congress leaders were largely unaware of the implications of the
abolition of the "Lame Duck Session."

It was also noted that only 20 per cent of the élite respondents
acknowledged any change in group influence within the Congress as a
result of the earlier election date (No. 4 above). Moreover, there was
a striking consensus that the members of the CPP should play the
pre-eminent role in selecting the Prime Minister (No. 5 above),
despite the near-universal acknowledgment of the Congress President's decisive role in all three contests and the widespread
knowledge of the important role played by the Chief Ministers in
1966, as well as the extensive bargaining which took place at that

time (No. 6 above). It appears, then, that the élite was uniform in its denial of extensive change in the relative influence of pressure groups within the Congress. They were also united in their desire to exclude all but the most essential groups from direct participation in the selection of the Indian Prime Minister. Stated in other terms, the élite as a whole focused heavily on the formal process of leadership selection.

Elite insight into the actual mechanics of selection was, however, much greater than the above would imply. The respondents overwhelmingly cited the Congress President as the most influential actor in all three succession contests, though they recommended that he be restricted to a marginal role. So too was the contrast between assessment and prescription regarding the Chief Ministers' role. Elite respondents were thus acutely aware of the informal and intricate processes of bargaining and consultation that characterized the succession contests. They sharply distinguished their preference for Prime Ministerial selection from reality.

It is possible that they underplayed the effects of specific events in the 1967 succession contest because of the extraordinarily high degree of consistency in their choice for Prime Minister throughout the crucial fortnight of negotiation. The choice of PM among the élite sample was fixed at least as early as the announcement of the General Election results at the end of February and was not appreciably influenced by the ensuing competition for support (No. 7 above). The stakes of the game were vital only to a few participants, and the modifications and compromises had little relevance beyond the inner core of Congress leaders. A substantial majority (70 per cent) expressed no doubt as to the outcome of a secret ballot: Mrs. Gandhi's victory was assured.

The indifference to specific events is also partly explained by the certainty of outcome. And the knowledge about the informal processes of negotiation is due to the intensive face-to-face contact between Congress rank-and-file and Congress leaders during the last two weeks. As noted, almost all the MPs discussed the contest with other members of the CPP; many also consulted national leaders, their Chief Minister, the Congress President, and their PCC President (No. 9 above). Thus, upward vertical communication was intense:

Congress MPs uniformly consulted Congress national leaders. In addition, the rank-and-file communicated horizontally with their own state governments. Congress leaders communicated vertically in a downward direction with Congress MPs; however, their horizontal contacts were sparse. In short, the only communication gap in this intricate network was between all-India leaders and leaders of their states. This is one index of advanced political development – at the all-India level.

The Congress rank-and-file were immersed in the succession struggle, but as objects of attention rather than as initiators of political action. Only one fourth of the MPs acknowledged that they had convened a meeting to discuss the succession with their colleagues. This supports the earlier observation that the succession contest, though involving all agencies of the Congress Party, was in essence a limited game, with a known outcome, and with few high-level active participants.

CHAPTER **6**

CONCLUSION

This inquiry into Indian élite attitudes has concentrated on two aspects of the political process — electoral behavior and leadership at the all-India level. Thus, any general conclusions to be drawn from the analysis must be regarded as tentative; they await similar explorations of related processes. Nevertheless, it is possible and desirable to place our findings in a theoretical framework for the analysis of political development.

Professor David Apter has suggested two ideal types of developing political systems — mobilization and reconciliation.[1] Mobilization systems attempt to mobilize political energies and resources to attack the problems of poverty, ignorance and economic backwardness. They seek to reconstruct society, both attitudes and institutions, in order to achieve material advance. Indeed, the underlying premise can be stated as a simple proposition: Economic progress is the basis for modern society. Mobilization systems are therefore characterized by hierarchical authority, total allegiance to the political system, tactical flexibility and ideological specialization. The political party or governmental apparatus serves as the central instrument of economic and social change.

The reconciliation system, by contrast, is a union of autonomous parts. It seeks a common denominator in order to satisfy all the important constituents of the political system. High priority is thus given to compromise among competing political and interest groups. Reconciliation systems are usually characterized by pyramidal authority structures, multiple loyalties, the acceptance of compromise, pluralism and ideological diffuseness.

In both system-types, economic development is a significant issue and a constant policy problem. Each uses a quite different strategy to cope with this demand. Economic development receives the highest priority in mobilization systems. Institutions are created to remove social obstacles to economic growth, and governmental enterprise becomes the main engineering path to development. In

[1] David Apter, "System, Process, and the Politics of Economic Development," J.L. Finkle and R.W. Gable (eds.), *Political Development and Social Change* (New York: John Wiley and Sons, 1966) pp. 441–57. The following delineation of the structure and process of the two types of political systems is based upon Apter's work.

reconciliation systems, however, economic objectives are more diffuse. The process of decision-making is less centralized, with the result that both the goal of economic development and progress toward its achievement are much more moderate. In mobilization systems, immediate satisfactions must be sacrificed for the sake of future benefits. In reconciliation systems, by contrast, possibilities for current savings are limited by the necessity for compromise between the demands of competing groups; there is a greater balance between developmental and system-maintenance decisions. In short, decision-making élites in reconciliation systems have a much more limited scope of action; a wider variety of constraints operates on development policies. In Apter's succinct formula, "mobilization systems fight society; reconciliation systems are prisoners of society."[2]

Apter's model can be readily applied to a study of Indian élite images of the political system. The perceptions of Congress respondents are typical of an élite operating within a reconciliation system. The attitudes of Opposition leaders and of nonpolitical respondents are more characteristic of an élite in a mobilization system.

Congressmen, that is, the incumbent Indian political élite, demonstrated a paramount concern with system-maintenance, not with development. They perceived deficiencies in the Congress party machine, dissidence, and factionalism as major factors in the outcome of the Fourth General Election.[3] The rank-and-file gave high priority to problems of national integration and party unity, and they were principally concerned with the continuing viability of the Congress as a political instrument. Finally, in their ranking of the requisite qualities for an Indian Prime Minister in the conditions of 1967, Congress respondents stressed Holding the Congress Together and Maintaining North-South Unity.[4]

[2] *Ibid.,* p. 451.
[3] See p. 39, No. 5 and p. 41 above.
[4] See p. 108, Nos. 2,3, and p. 111 above.

All this reveals a high priority of goals related to reconciliation and integration. Moreover, Congress MPs were preoccupied with the techniques of reconciliation: They focused on the integrative role, not on the transforming role of the Congress party in the Indian political system. Their sensitivity to the scope and impact of regional variations in the election outcome, to shifts in the authority structure of the party, and to changes in the personal and institutional loci of decision-making — all these are consistent with the supreme value they placed on political reconciliation and their image of the Congress as its indispensable instrument. Further, in the light of this emphasis on system-maintenance, the choice of Mrs. Gandhi was perfectly consistent. Nor is it surprising that the Congress setback at the polls led to a decline in the desire for change in Prime Minister.[5]

Opposition and nonpolitical élite images were, as noted, more typical of an élite functioning within a mobilization system. Their emphasis on the ability to cope with India's economic problems as a prime requisite for leadership reflects the priority given to economic development; indeed, non-Congress respondents perceived economic problems as the most important area of public policy.[6] Desai was rated very highly in his ability to deal with economic crises and to provide a better climate for business. He was, therefore, the logical candidate of those persons whose goals are of the mobilization type.

Two tables provide interesting evidence in support of these hypotheses. The first, Table 20, explores the consistency of élite attitudes to the choice of Prime Minister. Preliminary analysis of the data appears to indicate a striking inconsistency in choice: Fifty-five respondents ranked Economic Problems most important or second most important among the causes of the Congress setback in the 1967 General Election; a clear plurality of these persons ranked Morarji Desai as "best qualified" among the four Congress leaders to deal with Economic Problems; yet only 11 respondents (20 per cent) supported Desai for the Prime Ministership. The same zigzag pattern emerges from the data on Mrs. Gandhi: Only 9 of the 55 ranked her

[5] See p. 64, No. 7 and p. 66 above.

[6] See p. 108, No. 4 and p. 111 above.

TABLE 20

CONSISTENCY OF ELITE ATTITUDES TO CHOICE OF PRIME MINISTER

As noted in Table 2 : 2, *Economic Problems* occupied a position of pre-eminence in the assessment of general causes of the Congress setback in the Fourth General Election: 55 of the 80 respondents ranked it first or second in importance, 25 MPs and 30 Others.

Question: *How did these 55 persons rank the 4 Congress leaders in the Ability to Solve Economic Problems?*

	Mrs. Gandhi		Desai		Chavan		Kamaraj	
Rank 1	9	(4)[a]	25	(16)	8	(3)	13	(5)
Rank 2	6	(1)	6	(1)	11	(2)	5	(5)
Rank 3	10	(4)	3	(0)	4	(4)	2	(1)
Rank 4	22	(15)	12	(7)	23	(14)	24	(12)
No Rank	0	(0)	1	(0)	1	(1)	3	(1)
No Answer	8	(6)	8	(6)	8	(6)	8	(6)
TOTAL	55	(30)	55	(30)	55	(30)	55	(30)

[a]Figures in brackets refer to Others, i.e., non-Congress MPs, who comprised 30 of the 55 respondents.

Question: *Which candidate did these 55 respondents support for the Prime Ministership immediately after the General Election — and during the next two weeks?*

	Congress MPs	Others	Total
Mrs. Gandhi	16	12	28
Morarji Desai	5	6	11
Others	1	1	2
DUAC	1	5	6
No Answer	2	6	8
TOTAL	25	30	55

164

"best qualified" to cope with Economic Problems, 1 more than the lowest rated in this sphere, Chavan; more than 40 per cent of the respondents rated her "least qualified"; yet 28 of the 55 persons, or more than 50 per cent, supported her for the Prime Ministership. In group terms, the most pertinent comparison is the ranking and choice by Congress MPs who attached importance to Economic Problems in analyzing the election outcome: Five ranked Mrs. Gandhi first in her Ability to Solve Economic Problems, and 7 ranked her fourth; yet 16 of the 25 MPs supported her for the Prime Ministership. There were 9 MPs who ranked Desai first in this skill, and 5 who ranked him fourth; but only 5 supported him for the Prime Ministership. More pointedly, 8 MPs ranked Kamaraj most capable in the economic sphere, but only one MP favored him as Prime Minister.

The élite respondents, it is evident, did not transpose their analysis of the election results to their analysis and choice of the best qualified person for the position of Prime Minister. Several explanations may be suggested for this "gap." One is a discontinuity between the élite image of the kind of leadership required for an election campaign and the kind of leadership required for the country as Head of Government. Another is a discontinuity between élite recognition of the political significance of unsolved economic problems and the importance of economic skill in over-all leadership ability. A third theme, noted elsewhere in this study, is the widespread belief, expressed by many respondents, that India's economic problems are too massive in scope and are too deep-rooted for any leader to be able to solve them — alone. Thus other leadership qualities were regarded as more important in the choice of Prime Minister in 1967.

Another plausible hypothesis is that economic problems may be regarded by most foreigners and some Indians as the paramount task for India's leadership in the coming decades, but that ability in this sphere of policy is not pre-eminent among the Indian élite's criteria for choice of a Prime Minister. In other words, skill in economic matters does not outweigh *all* other skills in the composite image of élite respondents.

These explanations are compatible with each other. They also

reflect the underlying realities of the political process in reconciliation systems. Economic skills can never outweigh skills of
political bargaining and consensus-shaping. The apparent inconsist-
encies of élite attitudes to the choice of Prime Minister disappear
when economic development is treated as one of two or three
priority goals rather than the overriding objective of the system. It is
not surprising that the Congress rank-and-file, who are regional in
background, education, and interests, have the clearest and most
sharply attuned image of the reconciliation political process. The
success of Mrs. Gandhi's candidacy can best be interpreted, then, in
terms of her superior skill in bargaining and compromise.

TABLE 21

ELITE EXPECTATIONS ABOUT CENTER-STATE RELATIONS AFTER
THE 1967 GENERAL ELECTION

Question: *Do you expect the relations between Delhi and the State Governments to be characterized by greater tension, less tension, or no
change?*

	Congress MPs	Others	Total
Greater Tension	1	14	15
Less Tension	0	0	0
No Change	2	10	12
Uncertain (Don't Know)	1	2	3
No Answer[a]	32	18	50

[a]See note to Table 19 : 1.

Table 21 deals with élite expectations about center-state
relations after the Fourth General Election. The near-universal
expectation about future center-state relations was of greater tension
or continuation of the status quo; not a single respondent anticipated
a reduction of tension in the relations between Delhi and the states.
Within this nearly uniform consensus there were variations of group

emphasis. Only Cabinet Ministers expected a continuation of the status quo. All others — Working Committee members, Opposition leaders, Academics, and Journalists — predicted greater tension.

There is striking evidence here of the élite's acute awareness of the nature of reconciliation problems within the Indian political system. The consensus in anticipating an increase in federal-state tensions demonstrates the interplay and conflict between priority objectives. The comment of one Journalist, "secession, no, but real friction and tension within a year, yes; a real crisis of leadership now faces India," underlines the breadth and depth of disintegrative potentialities within the Indian polity. The necessity for allocation of scarce resources to system-maintenance (rather than development) increases proportionately with the scope and intensity of disintegrative demands.

The attribute of political sophistication, noted earlier, has been reinforced by this analysis. The Indian élite is composed largely of persons who are keenly aware of the nature of the reconciliation process and of the intricate and complex techniques of bargaining and compromise, which constitute its main features. A segment of the élite — Opposition leaders and communications specialists — have ordered their priorities differently, giving greater weight to the goal of rapid economic development. It is in this respect that they resemble their counterparts in mobilization systems. This is a healthy sign for the Indian body-politic because it reinforces incumbent élite awareness of the importance of economic growth.

Opposition and communications respondents probably attached greater weight to economic tasks because of their lack of practical and direct experience in the Indian policy-making process — until 1967. For this reason, too, it is likely that the images of Congress respondents are more congruent with the realities — both demands and constraints — of the decision-making process in all-India politics. Yet even the Opposition and the nonpolitical élites displayed extreme sensitivity to India's integrative problems.

During the first twenty years of independence, a relatively stable reconciliation system was sustained in India. The interaction between the two sets of élite images, different only in their order of priorities, produced a viable "mix" of development and system-maintenance decisions; the emphasis was clearly on stability.

APPENDIXES

QUESTIONNAIRE ON THE FOURTH GENERAL ELECTION,
LEADERSHIP, AND THE SUCCESSION OF 1967

A. *The Fourth General Election: Causes of the Congress Setback*

1. What do you think are the major factors that account for the failure of the Congress to do as well in this election as in the previous one? (Tables 2 : 1, 2 : 2)

Internal Quarrels among Groups Within the Party

The Absence of a Charismatic Leader like Nehru

Lack of Effective Leadership

Economic Problems

United Opposition

Others

Issues like Cow Slaughter, Language, etc.

2. Are the following factors, not mentioned by you in your initial comments, additional causes of the Congress setback? (Each factor was mentioned individually to each respondent.)   (Tables 2 : 3, 2 : 4)

Internal Quarrels

Issues Like Cow Slaughter

Lack of Effective Leadership

Absence of Charismatic Leadership

United Opposition

Economic Problems

3. Can you think of any specific action on the part of Government in the past year which has contributed to the decline of the Congress majority in Parliament and the Assemblies?   (Table 3 : 1)

None   Yes

4. Can you think of any specific action on the part of the Congress Party in the past year which has contributed to the decline of the Congress majority in Parliament and the Assemblies?   (Table 3 : 2)

None   Yes

B. *Role of Charisma, Personal Appeal, and Expectations*

    5. Do you think Mrs. Gandhi's position as the daughter of Jawaharlal Nehru helped the Congress Party in the Election?   (Table 4)

        Yes   No

    6. Did you, at any time during the past year (January 1966 to February 1967), think that another Prime Minister would have helped the party better in the Election?   (Table 5)

        Yes   No

    7. Were you surprised at the extent to which the Congress Party's fortunes declined in the recent General Election?   (Table 6)

        Yes   No

C. *The Fourth General Election: Effects of the Results*

    8. Do you think the results of the Election affected the balance of power between the party hierarchy and the parliamentary wing of the Congress?   (Table 7: 1)

        Yes   No

    9. Do you think the results affected the balance of power among the geographic groups within the Party?   (Table 7 : 2)

        Yes   No

  10. Did the results affect the balance of power between the Working Committee and the State Chief Ministers?   (Table 7 : 3)

        Yes   No

  11. What effects do you think the election results have had on the position of the Congress President relative to the following: (Table 7 : 4)

        Working Committee
        Congress Parliamentary Party
        State Chief Ministers
        Mrs. Gandhi
        Morarji Desai
        Y.B. Chavan

12. Do you think the election results benefited any candidate for the Prime Ministership? (Table 8)

    Yes   No

13. Did you, at any time during the year of Mrs. Gandhi's Prime Ministership, think it might be desirable to have a change of Prime Minister after the General Election? (Table 9 : 1)

    Yes   No

14. Did the election results make you feel that a change of leadership is desirable? (Table 9 : 2)

    Yes   No

D. *Qualities of Leadership: Assessment of Congress Candidates*

15. If you were given complete authority by the President to select a Prime Minister for India, what would you regard as the most important qualities for this post in the context of the current state of affairs? (Table 10)

    (The following were not mentioned by interviewer)

    National Image
    International Image
    Holding Congress Together
    Maintaining North-South Unity
    Satisfactory to Minorities
    Effective Leadership
    Strong Leader
    Flexible Leader
    Ability to Deal with Opposition in Parliament
    Ability to Deal with States
    Harmony with Party Leaders
    Implementation of Socialist Program
    Ability to Solve Economic Problems
    Providing a Better Climate for Business
    Pursuing a Successful Foreign Policy
    Others

16. Of the four Congress Leaders, Mrs. Gandhi, Desai, Chavan, and Kamaraj, whom would you regard as best qualified; second-best; third-best, and least qualified in—   (Tables 11 : 1 — 11 : 19)

    National Image

    International Image

    Holding Congress Together

    Maintaining North-South Unity

    Satisfactory to Minorities

    Effective Leadership

    Strong Leader

    Flexible Leader

    Ability to Deal with Opposition in Parliament

    Ability to Deal with States

    Harmony with Party Leaders

    Implementation of Socialist Program

    Ability to Solve Economic Problems

    Pursuing a Successful Foreign Policy

    Pursuing a Successful Policy

    Others

E. *The Succession Contest: 1967*

17. Do you think the decision to move forward the date of election of the Parliamentary Party Leader (from April 7 to March 12) was influenced by the election results?   (Table 12 : 1)

    Yes   No

    What factors other than the election results do you think affected that decision?

    1.

    2.

    3.

    4.

18. Who were the individuals most instrumental in making that decision?
(Table 12 : 2)

19. Do you think that this decision increased the chances of any particular candidate for the Prime Ministership? (Table 12 : 3)

    Yes   No

20. Did this decision affect the relative influence of groups (like State Chief Ministers, Parliamentary Party, Working Committee) in the choice of the Prime Minister? (Table 12 : 4)

    Yes   No

21. Did you think, at the time of Mrs. Gandhi's succession to Shastri, that it was a tentative choice made for the period until after the General Election?
(Table 13)

    Yes   No

22. Which of the following Congress agencies should participate in the *de facto* choice of the Prime Minister? (Table 14)

(a) CPP Executive   (d) Congress President

(b) CPP   (e) Chief Ministers

(c) Working Committee   (f) Pradesh Congress Committee Leaders

23. Which agency(ies) or person(s) played the crucial role(s) in the selection of the Prime Minister on this occasion? (Table 15 : 1)

(a)   CPP

(b)   Working Committee

(c)   Congress President

(d)   Chief Ministers

(e)   Syndicate

(f)   Others

24. Which agency(ies) or person(s) played the crucial role(s) in the succession contests of 1964 and 1966? (Table 15 : 2)

1964   (a)   Working Committee

       (b)   Congress President

       (c)   Chief Ministers

1966   (a)   CPP

       (b)   Congress President

       (c)   Chief Ministers

25. Which candidate did you support immediately after the General Election?

                                                                              (Table 16)
    Mrs. Gandhi

    Morarji Desai

    Others

Did you support the same candidate at the time of the CPP meeting to elect the Prime Minister?

    ·Yes   No

(To those who answered, "yes," to the above question) Did you at any time during the two weeks before the CPP meeting feel that another candidate might be better?

    Yes   No

26. Did you think that there was any question as to whether Mrs. Gandhi would win or not?
                                                                              (Table 17)

    Yes   No

By what majority did you think Mrs. Gandhi would win?

    100 or more than 100
    More than 50 but less than 100
    Less than 50

When did Mrs. Gandhi's victory become obvious to you?

    When Election Results Announced or Soon After
    Other

27. Did you, before the CPP meeting, discuss your voting and/or the leadership contest with the following?
                                                                              (Table 18 : 1)

(a)	Other Members of CPP	Yes	No
(b)	President of your PCC	Yes	No
(c)	Chief Minister of your State	Yes	No
(d)	Congress President	Yes	No
(e)	Other National Leaders	Yes	No

Were you a member of any group of CPP members who met formally or informally to decide on a common voting strategy?

Yes   No

28. Did you convene any meetings with Congress MPs or others during the two weeks before the election of the CPP Leader on 13 March?

(Table 18 : 2)

Yes   No

29. Were you satisfied or dissatisfied with the manner in which the new Cabinet was formed?   (Table 19 : 1)

Do you regard the composition of the new Cabinet as impressive or acceptable *or* unimpressive or unacceptable?

30. How long do you think the new Government will last, a full term of five years or less?   (Table 19 : 2)

31. (As noted in Table 2 : 2, *Economic Problems* occupied a position of pre-eminence in the assessment of general causes of the Congress setback in the Fourth General Election: 55 of the 80 respondents ranked it first or second in importance, 25 MPs and 30 Others.)

How did these 55 persons rank the 4 Congress leaders in the *Ability to Solve Economic Problems?*   (Table 20)

Mrs. Gandhi   Chavan
Desai   Kamaraj

Which candidate did these 55 respondents support for Prime Ministership immediately after the General Election — and during the next two weeks?

Mrs. Gandhi   Morarji Desai   Others

32. Do you expect the relations between Delhi and the State Governments to be characterized by greater tension, less tension, or no change?

(Table 21)

APPENDIX B

CAUSES OF CONGRESS SETBACK AT THE POLLS

PCCs' ASSESSMENT

FACTORS CITED IN ORDER OF IMPORTANCE

	Bihar	Haryana	Kerala	Madras	Mysore	Punjab	West Bengal	Delhi
Economic Discontent: Food	1	1	2	2	1	1	2	..
Prices	1	1	2	3	1	1	..	..
Corruption (Real or Alleged)	2	2	..	..	..	..	..	1
Cow Slaughter	7	1	..	..	..	3	..	..
United Opposition	..	..	1	1	..	..	..	..
Lack of Contact with Youth	8	..	..	..	9	..	..	..
Loss of Contact with People	..	..	..	..	..	..	1	..
Muslim Vote	9	..	..	..	..	..	..	..
Internal Congress Squabbles	10	4	..	..	4	2	..	..
Wrong Selection of Candidates	..	..	..	..	3	..	..	..
Other[a]	3–6	3	3	..	2, 5 – 8	4 – 8	3	2

Source: Typed document presented to the Working Committee of the Congress, "Preliminary Reports on Election Results From Some Pradesh Congress Committees." Made available to the author by a member of the Working Committee, March 1967.
[a] Other reasons indicated by the PCCs', in the order noted in Working Committee Document.

179

(Continued)

APPENDIX B – Continued

BIHAR 3 Atmosphere created by repeated calls of Bandhs and strikes by Opposition parties.
4 Atmosphere of terror created by Opposition parties.
5 Silencing of voters by threats and show of force.
6 Bogus voting.

HARYANA 3 Business community opposition.

KERALA 3 Opposition to President's Rule, which was identified with Congress.

MYSORE 2 Prohibition.
5 Hostility of Civil Servants.
6 Slow redress of grievances.
7 Widespread use of money by Opposition candidates.
8 Opposition of urban population.

PUNJAB 4 Formation of Punjabi Suba.
5 Delay in selection of Congress candidates because of fresh delimitation of constituencies.
6 Self-immolation threat of Sant Fateh Singh.
7 Refusal of all Ministers except the Chief Minister to campaign in any constituency but his own or to deposit electoral funds collected by them to PCC.
8 Hostility of Civil Servants – on communal basis.

WEST BENGAL 3 Refugee vote was anti-Congress.

DELHI 2 Faulty implementation of Master Plan, especially regarding housing.
Use of foreign money in support of "reactionary forces."

RANKING IN SEVEN STATES

Economic Discontent	ranked	first in Bihar, Haryana, Mysore, and Punjab, and second in Kerala, Madra, and West Bengal.
United Opposition	ranked	first in Kerala and Madras.
Corruption	ranked	first in Delhi, and second in Bihar and Haryana.
Cow Slaughter	ranked	first in Haryana (along with economic discontent), third in Punjab, and seventh in Bihar.
Internal Congress Squabbles	ranked	second in Punjab, fourth in Haryana and Mysore, and tenth in Bihar.

APPENDIX C

APPOINTMENT DIARY OF CONGRESS PRESIDENT KAMARAJ DURING THE SUCCESSION CONTEST 1967

A.M.	Sunday 26 Feb.	Monday 27 Feb.	Tuesday 28 Feb.	Wednesday 1 March	Thursday 2 March	Friday 3 March	Saturday 4 March
8:00							
8:30							
9:00							
9:30			D.N. Tiwari			Mrs. Sucheta Kripalani	
10:00			B.R. Bhagat			Mulgaonkar	V.K.R.V. Rao
10:30		– PARLIAMENTARY BOARD[a] –	Sushila Nayyar				
10:45			Atulya Ghosh[b]				
11:00			P. Govinda Menon	Brahm Parkash	M.C. Khanna		Rashtrapati Bhawan
11:30			Surjit Singh Majithia		Ram Kishen Gupta		
12:00	Arrival from Madras		Ram Krishna Hedge		Maharani Patiala		
12:30			Chandrasekharen			Atulya Ghosh[b]	Dimitrov (Bulg. A.)
12:45			D.R. Chavan				Jagjivan Ram[d]
1:00			Raghuram			Sanjiva Reddy[b]	Jagjivan Ram & Atulya Ghosh[b]
1:30							Prime Minister[c]
2:00							

182

P.M.	Sunday 26 Feb.	Monday 27 Feb.	Tuesday 28 Feb.	Wednesday 1 March	Thursday 2 March	Friday 3 March	Saturday 4 March
4:30					Mrs. V.L.Pandit		Sayeed Ali
5:00	Morarji Desai[c]		Ramachandran		Nanda[b]	Hitendra Desai[e]	S. Ali Zaheer
5:15	"				"	"	Mrs. S. Kripalani
5:30	"		B.K. Kaul			Ram Kishen	R. Varma
6:00	Prime Minister[c]		Khadilkar				Ranjit Singh
6:30	"		Swaran Singh[d]			C.M. Poonacha	S.D. Misra
7:00	Jagjivan Ram[d]	Working Committee[a]	Ram Subhag Singh[b]		Fakhruddin Ali Ahmed[d]	S.N. Sinha[d]	Channa Reddy Banarsidas
7:30	Doctor	Atulya Ghosh & Sanjiva Reddy[b]			Fakhruddin Ali Ahmed		Prime Minister[c]
8:00	Maharaja Patiala	Atulya Ghosh & Sanjiva Reddy	L.N. Mishra				Prime Minister
8:30	D.P. Mishra[e]		Patnaik[b]		Kamalapathi Tripathi		B. Reddy[e]
8:45	C.B. Gupta[e]		"				
9:00	Subramaniam		Nanda[b]		Musajir Subramaniam		V.P. Naik[e]
9:15			"				"
9:30	Nanda[b]		Chavan[d]		K.D. Malaviya		
10:00	Bhagwat Dayal		Chavan				
11:00							

(continued)

A.M.	Sunday 5 March	Monday 6 March	Tuesday 7 March	Wednesday 8 March	Thursday 9 March	Friday 10 March	Saturday 11 March
8:00							
8:30							
9:00					Sadiq		
9:15					Naik[e]		
9:30			Mrs. Jaipal Singh Tyagi	Nanda[b]	C.B. Gupta[e]		C.B. Gupta[e]
9:45				"	"		
10:00		Patnaik[b]		Jagjivan Ram[d]	WORKING	Sanjivan Reddy[b]	Nijalingappa[e]
10:15		Reddy & Ghosh[b]		Bhibuti Mishra		"	Morarji Desai[c]
10:30	Karanjia	Reddy & Ghosh		Sanjiva Reddy[b]	COMMITTEE	Desai/Prime M.[c]	25 MPs
10:45	"	Govind Sahay & Kamalapathi		Morarji Desai[c]		"	
11:00	Karanjia			Patnaik[b]		C.B. Gupta[e]	25 MPs
11:30	B.Mishra/Tiwari		Sanjiva Reddy[b]	Patnaik			Hanumanthaiya & V.K.R.V. Rao
11:45		S.K. Patil[b]		"			
12:00	B.R. Bhagat Mrs. T. Sinha	S.K. Patil		K.B. Sahay & R. Misra			B.R. Bhagat D.N. Tiwari
12:30	Brahmananda Reddy[e]	"	Jagjivan Ram[d]	Ram Lakan Singh	Atulya Ghosh[b]		K. Tiwari Bibhuti Mishra
1:00							
1:30							
4:00							

P.M.	Sunday 5 March	Monday 6 March	Tuesday 7 March	Wednesday 8 March	Thursday 9 March	Friday 10 March	Saturday 11 March
4:30				Venkataraman	Morarji Desai[c]		
4:45	Braham Parkash			Khandubhai Desai	„		
5:00	S.N. Sinha	Kamalapathi	Ram. S. Singh	Khadilkar		WORKING	
5:15	Ram K. Gupta	& Sahay	L.N. Misra			COMMITTEE	
5:30		V.K.R.V. Rao	Press	Sukhadia	Press		
6:00	Press	Press	Press	Prime Minister[c]	Nanda[b]	Morarji Desai & Prime Minister[c]	
6:15	„	„		Braham Parkash	„		
6:30				B. Reddy[e]		Morarji Desai & Prime Minister	
7:00			B.R. Bhagat	Press		D.P. Mishra[e]	
7:30	Atulya Ghosh[b]	S. Reddy[b]	Patthabi Raman	M.P. Sinha		C.B. Gupta[e]	
7:45						„	
8:00	S. Reddy[b]	S. Reddy	Venkataraman			C.B. Gupta	
8:30	Jaipal Singh					„	
9:00						B. Dayal Shamra & Rarewala	
9:30						„	
—							
11:00			Syndicate Reddy/Ghosh[b] Patil[b]/Gappa[e]				
12:00 midnite						Chavan[d]/Gupta[e] Mishra[e]/Ghosh[b] Patnaik[b]/D.Singh	

(Continued)

185

	Sunday 12 March	Monday 13 March
A.M.		
9:00–9:30		P.M. (with Cabinet List)[c]
11:00	Leader's Election	
P.M.		
5:00	Nanda[b]	

[a] Institutional Meetings

[b] Working Committee Members

[c] Contestants

[d] Cabinet Ministers

[e] Chief Ministers

INDEX

INDEX

ABOUT THE AUTHOR

Michael Brecher is presently a full professor of political science at McGill University where he also serves as Head of the South Asia Programme in the Centre for Developing-Area Studies. Since 1967, Dr. Brecher has been the McGill Representative on the Board of Directors for the Shastri Indo-Canadian Institute.

Fellowships from the Nuffield, Rockefeller and Guggenheim foundations and from the Canada Council have made it possible for Dr. Brecher to carry out extensive research in India and Pakistan, resulting in the publication of six major works (including *The New States of Asia* and *The Struggle for Kashmir*) as well as numerous articles dealing with Asian and international politics. His political biography *Nehru*, first published in 1959, was awarded the Watumull Prize of the American Historical Association in 1960 and has been printed in five languages, including Japanese.

Dr. Brecher received his doctorate in international relations from Yale University in 1953 and has taught at the University of Chicago and Yale. He is currently working on a major study of foreign policy.

DATE DUE

JAN 3 1999	JAN 0 5 1999	
GAYLORD		PRINTED IN U.S.A.